# Contents

**Contents**
Sensational Seasons: Winter, SV 9781419033964

# Introduction

Preschool curriculum and instruction have been dramatically affected by the federal legislation that demands that schools *Put Reading First* and *No Child Is Left Behind* in achieving reading and math skills. Currently, the most important instructional focus in preschool classrooms is literacy development—providing environments in which young children can explore words, language, books, and print through developmentally appropriate literacy events.

In a literacy-rich classroom, children are surrounded with print, and their days are filled with activities that invite them to interact with print. Children are encouraged to "pretend" or attempt to read and write. Their attempts at reading and writing emergently are honored and valued as children move through the stages of development to become conventional readers and writers. So, the preschool teacher's role has changed from one of getting children "ready" to read to one of getting children reading and writing.

## Activities Can Enrich Preschoolers' Literacy Experience

### First Page of Each Unit Provides:

- Book List
- Teacher Information (Facts)

### Second Page of Each Unit Provides:

- Illustrated Bulletin Board
- Materials List
- Teacher Preparation
- Student Directions

---

Sensational Seasons: Winter, SV 9781419033964

## Third and Fourth Pages Provide Circle Time Lessons That Include:

- Standard
- Lessons that include Language Arts, Math, and/or Science Skills
- Song or Poem

## Fifth Page of Each Unit Provides:

- Standard
- Writing Activity
- Simple Snack Idea

## Sixth and Seventh Pages Provide Center Ideas That Include:

- Standard
- Math Center Activity
- Language Center Activity
- Other Center Activities (Art, Science, Sensory)

## Remaining Pages of Each Unit Provide:

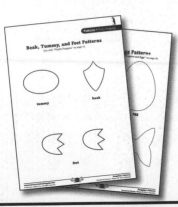

- Patterns and/or Activity Masters

# Standards

The following are preschool standards included with the activities and lessons in this book. Use these standards to guide further practice and to measure progress.

## Language Arts

| | Page(s) |
|---|---|
| Retells information from a story | 11, 38, 83 |
| Identifies some beginning sounds | 11, 83 |
| Demonstrates an understanding of letters and words | 11, 65 |
| Understands that reading progresses from left to right | 12, 84 |
| Uses scribbles, approximations of letters, or known letters to represent written language | 13, 51 |
| Begins to recognize high-frequency words | 14, 40, 86 |
| Recognizes and names rhyming words | 20, 32, 47, 57, 75 |
| Communicates information with others | 20, 87 |
| Shows awareness that different words begin with the same sound | 20, 30, 38, 68, 74 |
| Begins to distinguish words in sentences | 21, 66 |
| Makes illustrations to match sentences | 22 |
| Begins to identify letters of the alphabet | 23 |
| Predicts what will happen next using pictures and content for guides | 29, 47 |
| Begins to identify onsets and rimes | 29, 47 |
| Acts out plays, stories, or songs | 30, 48 |
| Writes to produce letters of the alphabet | 31, 33, 49, 69, 76 |
| Begins to distinguish letters in written text | 38, 50, 74 |
| Listens with understanding and responds to directions | 39, 49 |
| Begins to name the basic colors | 40 |
| Begins to understand alphabetical order | 41 |
| Understands that different text forms are used for different purposes | 31, 42, 67, 85 |
| Communicates ideas and thoughts | 56 |
| Begins to understand correct punctuation, capitalization, and sentence structure | 58 |
| Relates prior knowledge to new information | 65 |
| Follows two-step requests that are sequential but not related | 66 |
| Uses drawing and writing skills to convey meaning and information | 67 |
| Identifies letters in own name | 74 |
| Matches partner letters | 56, 59, 77 |
| Demonstrates some ability to hear separate syllables in words | 83 |

## Math

| | Page(s) |
|---|---|
| Draws common shapes | 12 |
| Counts objects using one-to-one correspondence | 13, 23, 24, 32, 50, 76, 86 |
| Describes and extends simple patterns | 14, 15, 78, 85 |
| Solves simple mathematical problems | 21, 84 |
| Uses measuring implements | 22, 69 |
| Sorts objects by one or two attributes | 29, 39, 65 |
| Recognizes and names numbers | 41, 68 |
| Begins to compare groups and recognize more than, less than, and equal to relationships | 48 |
| Uses positional terms such as in, on, over, or under | 57 |
| Names common shapes | 58 |
| Uses concepts that include number recognition and counting | 59 |
| Explores quantity and number | 75 |
| Begins to order objects in some attribute | 77 |

## Science

| | Page(s) |
|---|---|
| Uses senses to observe and explore materials | 60 |

## Art

| | Page(s) |
|---|---|
| Explores a variety of techniques to create original work | 15, 24, 42, 78, 87 |
| Explores a variety of materials to create original work | 33 |
| Uses responsible procedures in the care and use of materials | 51 |
| Explores a variety of tools to create original work | 60 |

Sensational Seasons: Winter, SV 9781419033964

# Rhyming Picture Cards

The following cards may be used as a center activity, allowing children to match rhyming word cards, sort the cards into categories, or make up silly rhymes using the rhyming word pairs.

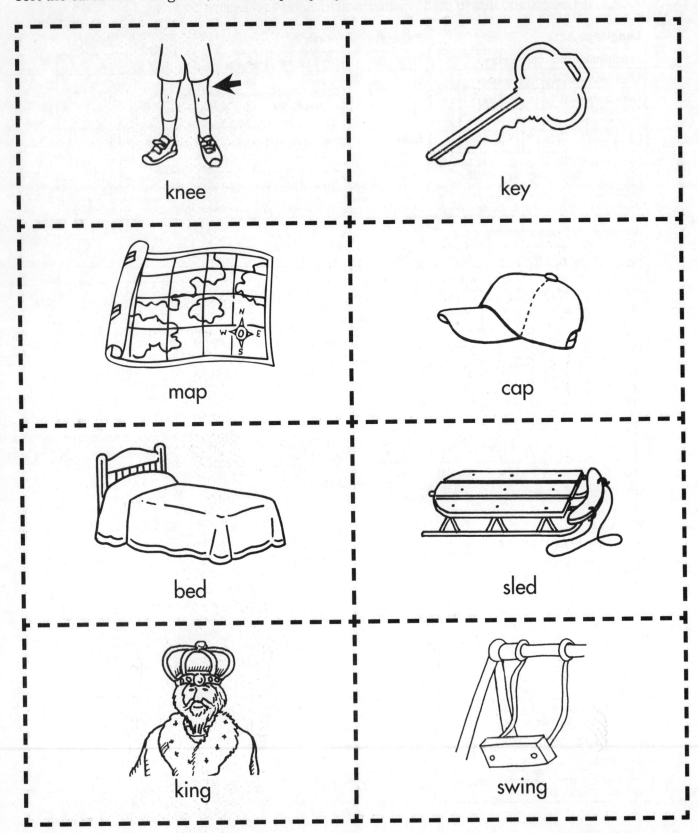

knee

key

map

cap

bed

sled

king

swing

# Rhyming Picture Cards

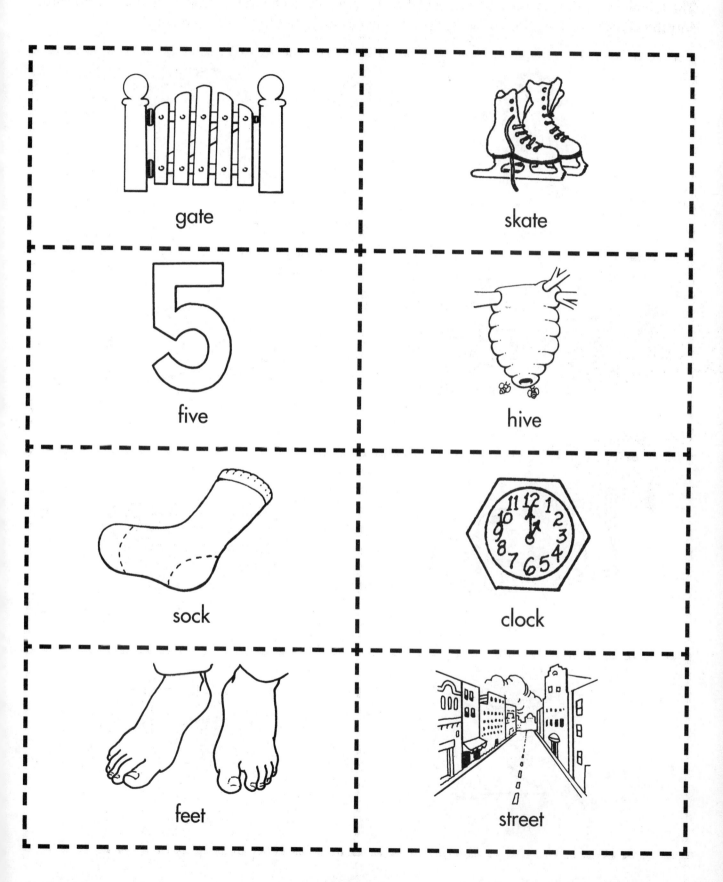

gate

skate

five

hive

sock

clock

feet

street

Rhyming Picture Cards
Sensational Seasons: Winter, SV 9781419033964

# Rhyming Picture Cards

fly

cry

frog

log

bug

mug

cut

nut

## Books to Read

*Festival of Lights: The Story of Hanukkah* by Maida Silverman (Aladdin Library)

*Grandma's Latkes* by Malka Drucker (Voyager Books)

*K Is for Kwanzaa: A Kwanzaa Alphabet Book* by Juwanda G. Ford (Cartwheel)

*My First Kwanzaa Book* by Deborah M. Newton Chocolate (Scholastic Paperbacks)

*Ten Christmas Sheep* by Nancy White Carlstrom (Eerdmans Books for Young Readers)

*The Magic Dreidels: A Hanukkah Story* by Eric A. Kimmel (Holiday House)

*The Night Before Christmas* by Jan Brett (Hodder Wayland)

*The Night of Las Posadas* by Tomie dePaola (Putnam Juvenile)

*The Wild Christmas Reindeer* by Jan Brett (Putnam Juvenile)

*Waiting for Christmas* by Monica Greenfield (Scholastic)

# Holiday Facts

During the winter months, people celebrate various holidays. Some holidays are religious, such as Hanukkah. It is a holiday that is celebrated by Jewish people and lasts for eight days. A candleholder called a menorah is a symbol of Hanukkah. A candle is lit for each of the eight days of Hanukkah, and gifts are exchanged and money given to the poor. Christmas started as a Christian holiday to celebrate the birth of Jesus. In many countries now, Christmas is a nonreligious holiday in which Santa Claus brings gifts for people to open on December 25. Many people decorate evergreen trees with lights and decorations during Christmas, and presents are put under the tree before they are exchanged. Kwanzaa is a nonreligious African-American holiday that is celebrated during the last seven days of December. Kwanzaa celebrates African-American traditions, community, family, and creativity.

# Holiday Happenings

## Materials

- craft paper
- border
- Christmas light pattern (p. 17)
- drawing paper
- markers or crayons
- large construction paper in holiday colors
- scissors
- glue
- stapler
- ribbon or yarn

## Directions

*Teacher Preparation:* Cover the bulletin board with craft paper. Add a border and the caption. Enlarge the Christmas light pattern and duplicate it multiple times to create a string of lights. Cut out and staple the lights in a pleasing arrangement around the drawings on the bulletin board. Add ribbon or yarn on the string of lights for the electrical cord. Provide each child with a strip of drawing paper on which to write a sentence.

1. Lead a discussion with children about how their families celebrate the holidays. Help children understand that all people do not celebrate the same holidays.

2. Have children write or dictate words that tell about one activity that their family does to celebrate Christmas, Hanukkah, or Kwanzaa.

3. Have children draw a picture to illustrate their sentence.

4. Have children frame their drawing and their sentence by gluing them on construction paper.

5. Staple the completed drawings in a pleasing arrangement around the Christmas lights on the bulletin board.

# Holiday Celebration Stories

***Language Arts Standard:*** *Retells information from a story*

- Select a story about a specific holiday celebration from the book list on page 9.
- Read the title and tell children the name of the author and the illustrator.
- Point out to children where the story starts and then read the book aloud.
- Invite children to retell the story by telling what happened at the beginning of the story, in the middle, and at the end.

# Giving the Gift

***Language Arts Standard:*** *Identifies some beginning sounds*

- Wrap a shoe box with holiday gift paper. Wrap the lid and box separately and stick a bow on the lid. Put small objects in the box that begin with familiar beginning sounds. You may wish to include holiday objects such as a bell, a toy tree, a bow, a candy cane, or a star.
- Have children sit in a circle and sing the following song to the tune of "Clementine" as they pass the gift around the circle.

  **Pass the gift, pass the gift.**
  **Pass the gift all around.**
  **When it stops, lift the lid**
  **And say the beginning sound.**

- Invite the child who is holding the gift when the word *stops* is sung to pick an object from the box.
- Challenge children to name the beginning sound of the object.
- Continue passing the box until all children have had a turn opening the box.

# Looking at Letters and Words

***Language Arts Standard:*** *Demonstrates an understanding of letters and words*

- Make two word cards for each child with the word *Christmas, Kwanzaa,* or *Hanukkah* on both of them. Leave about an inch between each letter. Give children the completed cards.
- Have children look at one word card and identify the beginning sound of the word.
- Have children count the letters in the word.
- Invite children to cut the letters apart on the second word card and mix them up.
- Encourage children to put the letters in the correct order to spell the word. Tell children that they may look at the first word card as a model.

Sensational Seasons: Winter, SV 9781419033964

# Shapes All Around

**Math Standard:** *Draws common shapes*

- Enlarge and duplicate the holiday shape cards (p. 16). Color and cut them out.
- Provide children with drawing paper and pencils or crayons.
- Challenge children to name the shape of the objects as the picture cards are shown one at a time.
- Have children draw the shape on their paper as each picture is shown. You may wish to draw the shapes ahead of time as a model for younger children to trace.

# In Tune with Language

**Language Arts Standard:** *Understands that reading progresses from left to right*

- Discuss with children how candles are often used during holiday celebrations.
- Depending on the holiday that the children are focusing on, write the words to the appropriate verse on a chart.
- Invite children to sing the following song to the tune of "Here We Go 'Round the Mulberry Bush."

**It's time to light the Kwanzaa candles,**
**The Kwanzaa candles, the Kwanzaa candles.**
**It's time to light the Kwanzaa candles**
**For seven nights in a row.**

**It's time to light the Hanukkah candles,**
**The Hanukkah candles, the Hanukkah candles.**
**It's time to light the Hanukkah candles**
**For eight nights in a row.**

**It's time to light the Christmas candles,**
**The Christmas candles, the Christmas candles.**
**It's time to light the Christmas candles**
**On this Christmas Eve.**

- Have children sing along as you point to the words in the song, emphasizing left to right progression.

# Let's Write: Holiday Greetings

**Language Arts Standard:** *Uses scribbles, approximations of letters, or known letters to represent written language*

- Lead a discussion with children about how people send or receive greeting cards during the holidays. Explain that sending a card is similar to sending a gift to someone they care about.

- Provide children with a generous supply of used holiday cards and inexpensive envelopes. Give them only the front section of the card that is decorated.

- Have children choose someone that they would like to give a card to. Then have them write a simple greeting and their name on the blank side of the card. Make a chart for the writing center that models greetings such as *Merry Christmas, Happy Kwanzaa,* or *Happy Hanukkah.*

- Invite children to fold the card, put it inside an envelope, and seal the envelope.

- Have them write the name of the person for whom the card is made. Accept scribble writing and letter approximations from younger children.

# Menorah Cracker

**Math Standard:** *Counts objects using one-to-one correspondence*

- Read children a book about Hanukkah that talks about the menorah. If possible, show them a real menorah.

- Have them count the eight candles on the menorah. Some menorahs have nine candles, and the center candle is the helper candle that is used to light each of the other candles for eight nights.

- Provide children with a tablespoon of peanut butter or cream cheese and a full graham cracker on a paper plate.

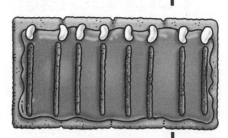

- Have children spread the peanut butter or cream cheese on the cracker using a jumbo craft stick.

- Invite children to lay eight pretzel sticks on the cracker for candles.

- Have children top each pretzel with a yellow jelly bean for the light.

- Encourage children to count their candles before eating the cracker.

**Caution: Be aware of children who may have food allergies.**

## Math Center

*Math Standard:*
*Describes and extends*
*simple patterns*

# Holiday Bracelets

- Discuss with children the traditional colors that are used for specific holiday celebrations. Use the colors listed in "Holiday Wrapping Paper" on page 15 as a guide.

- Provide children with pipe cleaners and with a generous supply of pony beads in the colors that apply to the holiday being studied. Younger children should use large beads on a string for safety.

- Invite children to put the beads on a pipe cleaner using a simple pattern such as the ones listed below.

**Christmas—red, red, green, green**
**Kwanzaa—red, green, black, red, green, black**
**Hanukkah—blue, yellow, yellow, blue, yellow, yellow**

- Help children twist the ends of the pipe cleaner together to make a bracelet.

- Encourage children to describe the pattern on their bracelet to a friend.

## Language Center

*Language Arts*
*Standard:*
*Begins to recognize*
*high-frequency words*

# Word Recognition

- Depending on the holiday focused on, duplicate several trees, dreidels, or ears of corn (p. 17) on construction paper.

- Write a high-frequency word such as *I, the,* or *is* on each cutout. Color the cutouts. Laminate them for durability and stick a piece of magnetic tape on the back of each one.

- Put the cutouts on a table with a set of magnetic letters and a cookie sheet.

- Invite children to put a tree, a dreidel, or an ear of corn on the cookie sheet. Use the magnetic letters to spell the high-frequency word written on the cutout.

- Challenge children to spell other words that are familiar to them.

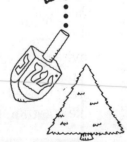

Sensational Seasons: Winter, SV 9781419033964

## Art Center

*Art Standard:*
*Explores a variety of*
*techniques to create*
*original work*

# Holiday Wrapping Paper

- Have children look through holiday books or magazines and find pictures of wrapped gifts.
- Discuss with children times when they have unwrapped gifts.
- Invite children to make wrapping paper for a holiday gift that they have made for a family member.
- Have them use a sponge to paint brown or white paper using the appropriate colors that signify the holiday celebrated in their home. Use the colors listed below as a guide.

**red and green for Christmas**
**red, green, and black for Kwanzaa**
**blue and yellow for Hanukkah**

## Sensory Center

*Math Standard:*
*Describes and extends*
*simple patterns*

# Candles in the Sand

- Put colored candles in the sand table. Include 9 white, 3 red, 3 green, and 1 black candle.
- Show children a menorah and a kinara. Use pictures if real ones are not available.
- Discuss with children the colors of the candles that are used on the menorah.
- Direct their attention to the order of the colors of the candles used on the kinara.
- Invite children to organize the candles in the correct color order and press them into the sand so they look like a menorah or a kinara.

# Holiday Shape Cards

Use with "Shapes All Around" on page 12.

# Christmas Light Pattern

Use with "Holiday Happenings" on page 10.

**light**

# Corn Pattern

Use with "Word Recognition" on page 14.

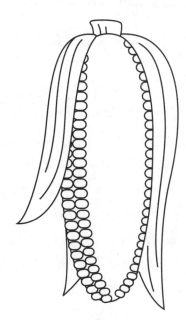

**corn**

# Dreidel Pattern

Use with "Word Recognition" on page 14.

**dreidel**

# Tree Pattern

Use with "Word Recognition" on page 14.

**tree**

## Books to Read

*A Little Bit of Winter* by Paul Stewart (HarperTrophy)

*Geraldine's Big Snow* by Holly Keller (Mulberry Books)

*Millions of Snowflakes* by Mary McKenna Siddals (Clarion Books)

*Sadie and the Snowman* by Allen Morgan (Scholastic Trade)

*Snowballs* by Lois Ehlert (Voyager Books)

*The First Snowfall* by Anne Rockwell (Aladdin)

*The Hat* by Jan Brett (Putnam Juvenile)

*The Jacket I Wear in the Snow* by Shirley Neitzel (Greenwillow)

*The Mitten* by Jan Brett (Putnam Juvenile)

*The Mitten* by Alvin Tresselt (HarperTrophy)

*There Was an Old Lady Who Swallowed Some Snow* by Lucille Colandro (Scholastic)

## Winter Facts

The winter season begins on December 21 and ends on March 20. During this time temperatures lower and days become shorter. Some plants die during the winter, while others stay alive through their root systems. Some animals, such as bears, hibernate during the winter because their food sources disappear at this time of year. Other animals, such as birds, migrate to a warmer climate during the winter months. Many animals adapt to winter weather by growing an extra layer of fur or feathers. Some animals turn a different color in the winter to protect themselves from predators.

# Brrr! It's Cold Outside

## Materials

- blue and white craft paper
- border
- large white construction paper
- tempera paints
- construction paper scraps
- yarn
- buttons
- paintbrushes
- scissors
- glue
- markers

## Directions

***Teacher Preparation:*** Cover the top one-third of the bulletin board with blue craft paper and the bottom two-thirds with white craft paper. Cut the top edge of the white paper so that it looks like snow-covered hills. Provide a large sheet of white construction paper for each child. Add a border and the caption.

1. Invite children to paint a circle for a head, with no hair or facial features.

2. Then have children paint a body dressed in warm winter clothes. Encourage them to include clothes such as a coat, mittens, and boots.

3. When the paint has dried, have children use paint or markers to add facial features to the head.

4. Invite children to glue strips of construction paper or yarn to the head for hair. Invite them to glue buttons on the coat.

5. Have children cut out a hat from construction paper and glue it on the head.

6. Cut out the paintings like paper dolls and staple them on the bulletin board in a pleasing arrangement.

# Matching Mittens

**Language Arts Standard:** *Recognizes and names rhyming words*

- Enlarge and cut out the mitten (p. 25) for use as a template.

- Trace and cut out several matching pairs of mittens from different patterns of wrapping paper or wallpaper.

- Duplicate a pair of rhyming word picture cards (p. 6) for each pair of mittens. Cut out the cards and glue one picture on the back of each mitten. Laminate the mittens for durability.

- Mix up the mittens and spread them out on the floor or on a table.

- Invite children to pick two mittens that match.

- Have them look at the picture on the back of the mittens and name the rhyming words.

- Challenge children to name a third word that rhymes with the pictures on their mittens.

# The Mitten

**Language Arts Standard:** *Communicates information with others*

- Read aloud to children the Jan Brett and Alvin Tresselt versions of *The Mitten*.

- Create a T-chart on the board to contrast the characters in the two stories.

- Invite children to name the characters in each version and write their responses on the chart.

| Jan Brett | Alvin Tresselt |
|---|---|
| boy named Nicki | boy |
| mole | mouse |
| rabbit | rabbit |
| hedgehog | owl |

# Looking at Letters and Words

**Language Arts Standard:** *Shows awareness that different words begin with the same sound*

- Write the word *winter* on the board, naming each letter as it is written. Point out that the word *winter* begins with the letter *Ww*.

- Have children find the letter *Ww* on the classroom alphabet picture cards. Talk about the key word picture that is used for *Ww*. The word begins with the same sound and letter as *winter*.

- Have children listen as you say word pairs. Invite them to shout "Wow" if both words begin with the /w/ sound. They should be silent if the words begin with different sounds.

| | |
|---|---|
| **winter-watermelon** | **winter-wish** |
| **winter-wake** | **winter-coat** |
| **winter-sled** | **winter-wagon** |

# How Many Snowflakes?

**Math Standard:** *Solves simple mathematical problems*

- Duplicate a counting board (p. 25) for each child. Have children color the tree brown and the sky blue.

- Provide each child with a small paper cup of mini-marshmallows to use as snowflakes.

- Invite children to count the correct number of "snowflakes" on their counting board to solve the following word problems. Have chidren eat the marshmallows when they have solved the problem.

   **There were 5 snowflakes on the ground. Two snowflakes melted. How many snowflakes were left?**

   **There were 4 snowflakes on the tree. There were 2 snowflakes on the ground. How many snowflakes were there altogether?**

   **There were 3 snowflakes falling from the sky. There were 3 more snowflakes on the ground. How many snowflakes were there altogether?**

- Continue with other word problems until the cup is empty.

# In Tune with Language

**Language Arts Standard:** *Begins to distinguish words in sentences*

- Write the words to the following song on a chart. Laminate the chart.

   **What can you do in the wintertime,**
   **The winter time, the wintertime?**
   **What can you do in the wintertime,**
   **The winter of the year?**

   **I'll ride my sled in the wintertime,**
   **The winter time, the wintertime.**
   **I'll ride my sled in the wintertime,**
   **The winter of the year.**

Repeat with other verses such as:

   **I'll use my skis...**
   **I'll jump in the snow...**
   **I'll use my skates...**

- Invite children to learn the song to the tune of "Here We Go 'Round the Mulberry Bush."

- Write the word *winter* on the chalkboard.

- Have children use a washable marker to find and circle the word *winter* on the chart within the words of the song.

- Have them count how many times the word *winter* is used in the song.

Sensational Seasons: Winter, SV 9781419033964

# Let's Write: Class Book About Snow

**Language Arts Standard:** *Makes illustrations to match sentences*

- Write the following sentence frame on a sentence strip.

  **Snow is on the** _____ .

- Challenge children to complete the sentence by writing or dictating it on a sheet of drawing paper following left to right progression.

- Have children draw an illustration to go with their sentence.

- Staple the drawings together and add a cover to make a class book. Title the book *Snow*.

# Snowflake Pancakes

**Math Standard:** *Uses measuring implements*

- Using a package mix, prepare pancake batter as directed. Lead a discussion with children about the importance of measuring each ingredient. Invite children to help measure and mix the ingredients.

- Out of reach of children, pour the batter on a griddle and cook until brown.

- Provide each child with at least one pancake.

- Have children place a small doily on top of their pancake.

- Invite them to use a flour sifter to sprinkle powdered sugar on their pancake.

- Have children carefully lift the doily to reveal a snowflake pattern.

- Invite them to eat their pancake with a fork or with their hands.

**Caution: Be aware of children who may have food allergies.**

## Math Center

*Math Standard:*
Counts objects using one-to-one correspondence

# Snowman Button Counting

- Duplicate ten snowmen and ten hats (p. 26). Color the hats, scarves, and other details with crayons. Write a number from 1 to 10 on each of the hats. Cut out the hats and laminate them.

- Provide a generous supply of buttons or pompoms for counting.

- Invite children to identify the number on each snowman's hat.

- Then have children count the corresponding number of buttons or pompoms and place them on each snowman.

## Language Center

*Language Arts Standard:*
Begins to identify letters of the alphabet

# Snowflake Beanbag Toss

- Paint 8 to 10 large snowflakes on a four-by-four-foot sheet of blue craft paper. Use a black marker to write a target letter on each snowflake.

- Tape the paper securely to the floor. Place a line of tape about four or five feet from the paper for children to stand behind to play the game.

- Invite children to stand behind the tape and toss a beanbag so that it lands on a snowflake.

- Have children name the letter that the beanbag lands on. For phonemic awareness, have children name a word that begins with that sound.

- If desired, children can play with partners and keep score by snapping together plastic cubes each time they name the letter correctly.

Sensational Seasons: Winter, SV 9781419033964

## Art Center

*Art Standard:*
Explores a variety of
techniques to create
original work

# Snowman Art

- Set up a paint center with white paint and blue construction paper.

- Invite children to dip the end of an empty thread spool in the paint and use it as a snowflake stamp. Have children cover the blue paper with snowflakes.

- Then have children paint snow on the ground and paint a snowman.

- While the paint is still wet, have children sprinkle Epsom salts over the paper. The salt will give the "snow" a sparkly effect.

- When the paint has dried, have children use markers to draw details on the snowman. Have them include a hat, a scarf, buttons, and facial features.

## Sensory Center

*Math Standard:*
Counts objects
using one-to-one
correspondence

# Snow and Ice

- Fill the sensory tub with flour and clear, smooth stones that can be purchased from the floral department of any craft-supply store. Also, make available measuring cups, a sifter, slotted spoons, and an empty egg carton.

- Write a number in the bottom of each cup in the egg carton. For younger children, repeat familiar numbers.

- Invite children to use the spoons to find the "ice" that is hidden in the "snow."

- Encourage children to count the correct number of stones and place them in the egg carton cups.

# Mitten Pattern

Use with "Matching Mittens" on page 20.

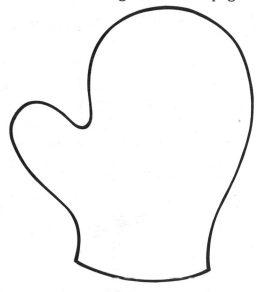

**mitten**

# Winter Scene Counting Board

Use with "How Many Snowflakes?" on page 21.

Sensational Seasons: Winter, SV 9781419033964

# Snowman and Hat Patterns
Use with "Snowman Button Counting" on page 23.

**hat**

**snowman**

# Castles in the Kingdom

## Books to Read

*A Medieval Feast* by Aliki (HarperTrophy)

*Get Well, Good Knight* by Shelley Moore Thomas (Puffin)

*Good Night, Good Knight* by Shelley Moore Thomas (Puffin)

*King Bidgood's in the Bathtub* by Audrey Wood (Harcourt Children's Books)

*Knights in Shining Armor* by Gail Gibbons (Little, Brown Young Readers)

*Prince Cinders* by Babette Cole (Putnam Juvenile)

*Princesses Are Not Quitters!* by Kate Lum (Bloomsbury USA Children's Books)

*The Knight and the Dragon* by Tomie dePaola (Putnam Juvenile)

*The Paper Bag Princess* by Robert N. Munsch (Annick Press)

*The Tale of Custard the Dragon* by Ogden Nash (Little, Brown Young Readers)

## Castle Facts

Royalty is the extended family of a monarch. Typically, the head of a royal family is a king or queen. During the Middle Ages, royal families needed help in waging war and protecting their land. So they gave bits of land to other nobility such as lords or knights. The royal family lived in a castle which served as a fortress, as a residence for their family and servants, and as a means of preserving the rigid hierarchy of the times. A common design of a castle included a moat with a drawbridge and a high stone wall for protection. Life within the walls of the castle was self-sufficient. Meals were one of the only forms of entertainment during this period.

# Our Preschool Coat of Arms

## Materials

- craft paper
- border
- shield pattern (p. 34)
- markers
- ruler
- black permanent marker
- white construction paper or poster board
- scissors
- stapler

## Directions

***Teacher Preparation:*** Enlarge the shield pattern to desired size. Cut it out for use as a template. Trace a shield for each child on construction paper or poster board. Use a black marker and a ruler to draw lines that divide the shield into four sections. Add a border and the caption.

Explain to children that a coat of arms looks like a shield and that the pictures on it tell various things about a person and his or her family.

1. Have children draw a picture of themselves in the first section of the coat of arms. Have them write their name in the section.

2. Invite children to draw a picture of the people in their family in the second section.

3. Have children draw a picture of a pet or a favorite animal in the third section. Have children label the drawing with the pet's name or the name of the animal.

4. Invite children to draw a picture of their school in the fourth section. Tell children to label the drawing with the name of the school.

5. Have children cut out their completed coat of arms.

6. Staple the coats of arms in a pleasing arrangement on the bulletin board.

# Making Predictions

**Language Arts Standard:** *Predicts what will happen next using pictures and content for guides*

- Read aloud a book from the list on page 27, such as *The Paper Bag Princess* by Robert N. Munsch or *The Knight and the Dragon* by Tomie dePaola.

- Have children predict what will happen before reading the end of the story.

- Encourage them to look at the illustrations to help with their predictions.

- Have children retell the story to check for levels of comprehension.

# Count the King's Money

**Math Standard:** *Sorts objects by one or two attributes*

- Discuss with children how kings and other nobility had lots of money. Tell them that in medieval times, gold was the accepted form of money, but today we use different kinds of coins as money.

- Show them a penny, nickel, dime, and quarter. Name the coins and discuss the size and color of each coin.

- Collect a generous supply of real coins to use as "the king's money." Put a handful of coins, including at least one of each, in a clean, child-sized tube sock. Provide a sock "money bag" for each child.

- Place a large sorting tray in the middle of the rug. Have children sit in a circle around the tray.

- Invite children to help count the king's money by sorting the coins in the tray.

# Looking at Letters and Words

**Language Arts Standard:** *Begins to identify onsets and rimes*

- Say the following words, separating the onset and rime.

  **k-ing**
  **qu-een**
  **c-astle**
  **kn-ight**
  **dr-agon**
  **g-old**

- Invite children to blend the sounds together and say each word.

# The Paper Bag Princess Words

***Language Arts Standard:*** *Shows awareness that different words begin with the same sound*

- Read aloud *The Paper Bag Princess* by Robert N. Munsch.
- Cut the seams on seven plain, brown grocery bags from top to bottom. Cut a hole for the neck and two armholes from the sides.
- Write one letter on the flat side of each bag with a black marker. Use the letters *b, g, a, e, i, o,* and *u.*
- Invite seven children to put on a paper bag with the letters in the front to resemble the princess (or prince) in the story.
- Have children wearing *b, a,* and *g* stand together. Have the other children sound out the letters to read the word *bag.*
- Have the child wearing the letter *e* replace the letter *a.* Have the other children sound out the letters to read the word *beg.*
- Continue using all of the vowels to spell *big, bog,* and *bug.*
- List the words on the board so that children can read the words again.

# In Tune with Language

***Language Arts Standard:*** *Acts out plays, stories, or songs*

- Have children learn the nursery rhyme "Old King Cole."

  **Old King Cole was a merry old soul**
  **And a merry old soul was he.**
  **He called for his pipe,**
  **And he called for his bowl,**
  **And he called for his fiddlers three.**

- Have a child wear a crown and be "Old King Cole." Have three other children be the fiddlers. Provide a bubble pipe and a bowl as props.

- Invite children to pantomime the rhyme.

Sensational Seasons: Winter, SV 9781419033964

# Let's Write: Writing with Flavor

**Language Arts Standard:** *Writes to produce letters of the alphabet*

- Show children a salt shaker. Lead discussion with them about how salt is sprinkled on food to give it flavor.

- Explain to children that in medieval times, kings and other royalty had saltcellars. These small containers held salt for them to flavor their food. If possible, show them a real saltcellar.

- Fill a shoe box lid about half full of salt. Place the shoe box lid on a cookie sheet with sides for easier cleanup.

- Make a set of word cards with royal words such as *king, queen, knight, dragon,* and *castle.* You may wish to make letter cards for younger children.

- Invite children to use their finger to write the words in the salt. Have them smooth over the salt with their hand to erase each word.

# A Royal Feast

**Language Arts Standard:** *Understands that different text forms are used for different purposes*

- Read aloud *A Medieval Feast* by Aliki, which tells about a lord and lady preparing for a visit by the king and queen. The book helps children understand that meal preparation was very different during medieval times.

- Have children make and send an invitation to the "king" or "queen" of the school to attend the feast. This could be any adult who works in the school such as the principal or director.

- Have children help cover a large table with clean, white paper. Explain that many meals were eaten with no plates during medieval times.

- Then have children help prepare several finger foods. They can cut cheese into cubes, wash grapes, and put bread slices on plates.

- Have children place all of the foods on plates or in baskets and set them in the middle of the table.

- Finally, when the "king" or "queen" arrives, demonstrate how to pass the food around the table to everyone. Have children eat their meal with their hands. Remember to have children wash their hands thoroughly before eating.

**Caution: Be aware of children who may have food allergies.**

**Castles: Writing Activity and Snack Idea**
Sensational Seasons: Winter, SV 9781419033964

## Math Center

***Math Standard:***
*Counts objects using one-to-one correspondence*

# The Crown Jewels

- Duplicate the crown (p. 34) for use as a template. Trace ten crowns on file folders and cut them out. Cover each crown with gold wrapping paper or aluminum foil. Write a number from 1 to 10 on each crown using a permanent marker.

- Provide a generous supply of smooth, colored gemstones that can be purchased from the floral department of any craft-supply store.

- Invite children to decorate the crowns with jewels by putting the correct number on each crown.

## Language Center

***Language Arts Standard:***
*Recognizes and names rhyming words*

# Rhyming Memory Game

- Duplicate four pairs of rhyming picture cards (pages 6–8). Cut them out and glue each one on an index card.

- Purchase eight plain cone-shaped party hats. Invite children to help decorate the hats with glitter, jewels, and streamers to resemble princess hats. Cone hats can also be made from construction paper, if desired.

- Mix up the rhyming cards and lay them in two equal rows. Cover each card with a princess hat.

- Challenge children to lift two hats at a time. If the two picture cards rhyme, have them keep the cards in a pile. If the cards do not rhyme, have them cover the cards with the hats.

- Have children continue playing until all of the cards are matched.

## Art Center

*Art Standard:*
*Explores a variety of*
*materials to create*
*original work*

# Accordion Dragon

- Duplicate the dragon head and tail (p. 35) on green construction paper for each child.

- Provide each child with a half sheet of green construction paper that has been cut lengthwise. Accordion fold the paper.

- Invite children to cut out the head and tail of the dragon.

- Have children decorate the dragon with dots of paint, sequins, or markers.

- Help children glue one end of the folded paper to the head and the other end to the tail.

- Have children tape one straw to the head and one straw to the tail to use as handles.

## Sensory Center

*Language Arts*
*Standard:*
*Writes to produce*
*letters of the alphabet*

# Building Castles

- Slightly dampen the sand in the sand table with a spray water bottle.

- Invite children to build a sand castle using plastic buckets, shovels, or other sand toys.

- Encourage children to add windows, turrets, and a moat around the castle.

- Have children use a small piece of cardboard for a bridge across the moat.

- Have children make flags by cutting triangles from construction paper and gluing them to craft sticks.

- Then have children write the first letter of their name on the flag and put it on top of the castle.

# Shield Pattern
Use with "Our Preschool Coat of Arms" on page 28.

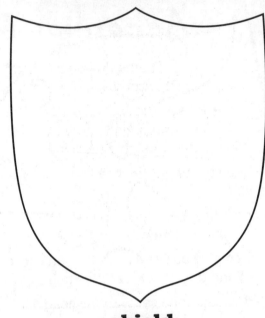

**shield**

# Crown Pattern
Use with "The Crown Jewels" on page 32.

**crown**

Sensational Seasons: Winter, SV 9781419033964

# Dragon Pattern

Use with "Accordion Dragon" on page 33.

**dragon**

Sensational Seasons: Winter, SV 9781419033964

## Books to Read

*Big Old Bones: A Dinosaur Tale* by Carol Carrick (Clarion Books)

*Can I Have a Stegosaurus, Mom? Can I? Please!?* by Lois G. Grambling (Troll Communications)

*Dazzle the Dinosaur* by Marcus Pfister (North-South)

*Digging Up Dinosaurs* by Aliki (HarperCollins)

*Dinosaurumpus!* by Tony Mitton (Orchard)

*How Do Dinosaurs Get Well Soon?* by Jane Yolen (Blue Sky Press)

*How Do Dinosaurs Say Good Night?* by Jane Yolen (Blue Sky Press)

*My Dinosaur* by Mark Alan Weatherby (Scholastic)

*Saturday Night at the Dinosaur Stomp* by Carol Diggory Shields (Candlewick)

*The Big Book of Dinosaurs: A First Book for Young Children* by Angela Wilkes (DK Children)

# Dinosaur Facts

Over 500 kinds of dinosaurs have been discovered that lived during the Mesozoic Era. This era was divided into three periods: the Triassic, Jurassic, and Cretaceous. Although the blue whale is bigger than a sauropod, the plant-eating sauropods were the largest animals to ever walk the earth. Most dinosaurs were plant eaters that walked on four legs. Some were meat eaters that walked on two muscular hind legs that provided speed for catching their prey. The largest dinosaurs were over 100 feet long and up to 50 feet tall, while the smallest was the size of a chicken. Scientists believe all dinosaurs hatched from eggs. The gigantic sauropods laid eggs about the size of a volleyball. Dinosaurs became extinct some 65 million years ago.

 Sensational Seasons: Winter, SV 9781419033964

# My Name Is Stegosaurus

## Materials

- dinosaur pattern (p. 43)
- blue craft paper
- white construction paper
- border
- tempera paints
- sponges
- clothespins
- wiggly eyes
- paintbrushes
- dish or plate for each paint color
- glue
- scissors
- stapler

## Directions

**Teacher Preparation:** Duplicate a dinosaur for each child on white construction paper. Cut the sponges into small squares and clip each square with a clothespin. Put paints in dishes or plates. Add a border and the caption.

1. Have each child cut out a dinosaur. Younger children may need help with cutting.

2. Have children dip the sponge into the paint and press it onto the dinosaur in a random pattern. Children may add other colors if desired.

3. Have each child glue a wiggly eye on his or her dinosaur.

4. Invite children to paint a background mural on the blue craft paper. Encourage them to include trees, mountains, a river, and a volcano.

5. Staple the dinosaurs on the bulletin board in a pleasing arrangement.

# Paleontologists On the Go

**Language Arts Standard:** *Retells information from a story*

- Fill a backpack with items that a paleontologist might use, such as safety goggles, a small hammer, a chisel, a whisk broom, gauze (plaster wrap for fossils), a toy camera, a notepad and pencil, and a small box. If possible, include a real fossil or make one by pressing a toy dinosaur in clay to make an imprint.

- Show children the backpack and remove all of the items for them to see.

- Tell them that you want to be a paleontologist but you don't know what to do with all of the things in the backpack.

- Read aloud a book such as *Digging Up Dinosaurs* by Aliki that shows the process of fossil hunting.

- Invite children to tell how the items from the backpack were used in the book.

# Saurus Means Lizard

**Language Arts Standard:** *Begins to distinguish letters in written text*

- Write the words *Apatosaurus, Stegosaurus, Tyrannosaurus,* and *Brachiosaurus* on a chart. Tell children that these are dinosaur names. Add other similar names to the list if desired.

- Invite children to look at the last letter of each name. Ask them to tell if it is the same letter or a different letter.

- Challenge them to compare the words and find other letters that are the same.

- Have a volunteer draw a line under all of the letters that are the same in each word.

- Explain to children that *saurus* means lizard.

# Looking at Letters and Words

**Language Arts Standard:** *Shows awareness that different words begin with the same sound*

- Collect several objects whose names begin with the letters *Dd* and *Ff,* such as a dime, a toy dog, a doll, a duck, a feather, a flag, a football, or a flower. Put the objects in a box or bag.

- Write the words *Dinosaur* and *Fossil* on the board, naming each letter as it is written.

- Have children find the letters *Dd* and *Ff* on the classroom alphabet picture cards. Talk about the key word picture that is used for each letter. Tell children that the names of the pictures begin with the same sounds and letters as *Dinosaur* and *Fossil.*

- Invite children to pick an item from the box or bag and tell if its name begins with the same sound as *Dinosaur* or *Fossil.*

- Make a list on the board of the words that begin with each sound.

# Herbivores or Carnivores

**Math Standard:** *Sorts objects by one or two attributes*

- Make a large nest using a brown sheet or brown fabric. Put the nest on a rug so that children can sit around it.

- Prepare an egg for each child by putting a small plastic dinosaur inside a white plastic egg. Arrange the eggs in the nest.

- Label two shallow containers with the word *Herbivore* on one and the word *Carnivore* on the other. Draw a picture of a plant or some kind of meat next to each word to illustrate it.

- Lead a discussion with children about how most dinosaurs that ate plants walked on four legs and dinosaurs that ate meat walked on two legs. Show children pictures of plant eaters that show their flat teeth and pictures of meat eaters that show their sharp teeth. Introduce children to the words *Herbivore* and *Carnivore*.

- Invite children to take an egg from the nest and open it.

- Encourage them to tell if the dinosaur was a plant eater or a meat eater. Younger children may need guidance.

- Have children place the dinosaur in the correct container, according to what it ate.

- If desired, have children count and compare the sets of dinosaurs.

# In Tune with Language

**Language Arts Standard:** *Listens with understanding and responds to directions*

- Duplicate a set of dinosaurs (p. 44) for each child.

- Invite children to learn the following song to the tune of "London Bridge."

  **I can find a dinosaur,**
  **Dinosaur, dinosaur.**
  **I can find a dinosaur**
  **That has sharp, sharp teeth.**

Repeat with other verses such as:

  **…that has a long neck.**
  **…that has three sharp horns.**
  **…that has bony plates.**

- Have children point to the correct dinosaur as each verse is sung.

# Let's Write: Going On a Word Dig

***Language Arts Standard:*** *Begins to recognize high-frequency words*

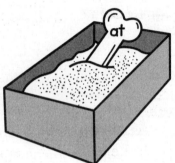

- Duplicate several bones (p. 43) on white construction paper. Cut them out and write a familiar sight word such as *I, and, the,* or *at* on each bone. Laminate the bones for durability.

- Bury the "bones" in a shallow tub of sand. Place the tub near the writing table.

- Provide children with plain writing paper and pencils.

- Encourage children to be paleontologists and dig up the "bones."

- Have children record their findings by writing the sight words that are on the bones on their paper.

# Pudding Fossils

***Language Arts Standard:*** *Begins to name the basic colors*

- Prepare chocolate pudding according to package directions.

- Crush cream-filled chocolate cookies in a zippered plastic bag. Pour the crushed cookies in a bowl with a spoon.

- Provide each child with a clear plastic cup that is half full of pudding, five or six dinosaur fruit snacks, and a spoon.

- Invite children to stir one spoonful of crushed cookies into their pudding.

- Then have children stir in the dinosaur fruit pieces.

- Encourage children to use their spoon to dig out the dinosaurs and then name the color of each one.

**Caution: Be aware of children who may have food allergies.**

Sensational Seasons: Winter, SV 9781419033964

## Math Center

*Math Standard:*
*Recognizes and names numbers*

# Dinosaur Footprints

- Draw ten large dinosaur footprints on brown paper. Make them about twelve inches square.

- Cut them out and write a number from 1 to 10 on each one. Laminate them for durability.

- Tape the footprints on the floor to resemble dinosaur tracks.

- Invite children to stand on the number 1 and name the numbers as they follow the tracks.

- For a more challenging activity, tape the tracks on the floor with the numbers in random order.

## Language Center

*Language Arts Standard:*
*Begins to understand alphabetical order*

# ABC Stegosaurus

- Enlarge and duplicate the stegosaurus (p. 43) on green construction paper. Cut off all of the bony plates. Write a letter *A* through *F* on each of the plates. Laminate the body and the plates separately. Cut them out.

- Write the alphabet on a sentence strip for children to use as a guide.

- Invite children to arrange the plates across the back of the stegosaurus in alphabetical order.

- Challenge children to arrange any six sequential letters of the alphabet across the back of the stegosaurus.

Sensational Seasons: Winter, SV 9781419033964

## Art Center

*Art Standard:*
*Explores a variety of techniques to create original work*

# Shape-o-saurus

• Provide each child with a sheet of drawing paper that has a large circle, triangle, square, rectangle, or oval drawn in the center of the paper. Use a permanent black marker to draw the shape.

• Have children turn their shape into a dinosaur by using crayons or markers to add body parts and features.

• Invite children to add texture to their dinosaur by using various craft items such as glitter, yarn, buttons, and construction paper.

• Encourage children to draw a background for their dinosaur picture.

## Science Center

*Language Arts Standard:*
*Understands that different text forms are used for different purposes*

# Looking Up Dinosaurs

• Provide several medium-sized plastic dinosaurs and one or two informational picture books about dinosaurs at the science table.

• Invite children to look at a plastic dinosaur closely and notice any unusual characteristics that it might have.

• Have children find a picture of the dinosaur in one of the picture books.

• Encourage children to ask questions about the dinosaurs. Help them use the books to find answers to their questions.

# Stegosaurus Pattern

Use with "My Name Is Stegosaurus" on page 37 and "ABC Stegosaurus" on page 41.

## stegosaurus

# Bone Pattern

Use with "Going On a Word Dig" on page 40.

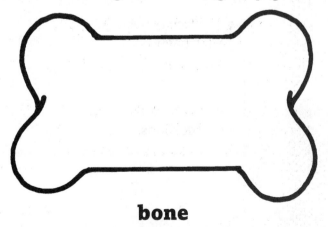

**bone**

Sensational Seasons: Winter, SV 9781419033964

# Dinosaur Patterns

Use with "In Tune with Language" on page 39.

**apatosaurus/brontosaurus**          **stegosaurus**

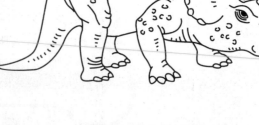

**tyrannosaurus**          **triceratops**

**Dinosaurs: Patterns**
Sensational Seasons: Winter, SV 9781419033964

## Books to Read

*A Birthday for Frances* by Russell Hoban (HarperTrophy)

*Arthur's Birthday* by Marc Brown (Little, Brown Young Readers)

*Carl's Birthday* by Alexandra Day (Farrar, Straus & Giroux)

*Clifford's Birthday Party* by Norman Bridwell (Cartwheel)

*Happy Birthday to You!* by Dr. Seuss (Random House Books for Young Readers)

*It's My Birthday* by Helen Oxenbury (Candlewick)

*Some Birthday!* by Patricia Polacco (Aladdin)

*The M&M's Brand Birthday Book* by Barbara Barbieri McGrath (Charlesbridge Publishing)

*The Secret Birthday Message* by Eric Carle (HarperTrophy)

## Birthday Facts

Birthdays were originally celebrated only by prominent men in a country. However, today birthdays are celebrated by young and old alike all around the world. Customs vary from country to country. Many children in the United States have birthday parties with a cake and candles. The origin of birthday parties goes back to when people believed that good and evil spirits appeared when children were born and influenced them for their entire life. People also believed that having a party with friends and family would scare the evil spirits away. The custom of putting candles on the cake originated about 200 years ago in Germany. Germans were excellent candle makers and began making tiny candles that were put on a birthday cake. They came up with the idea that it was good luck to blow out all of the candles at the same time.

Sensational Seasons: Winter, SV 9781419033964

# We Shine on Our Birthdays

## Materials

- craft paper
- border
- twelve blank word cards
- permanent markers
- empty bathroom tissue rolls
- yellow tissue paper
- tempera paint
- clothespins
- paintbrushes
- glitter in a shaker bottle
- blank index cards
- glue or tape
- scissors
- stapler

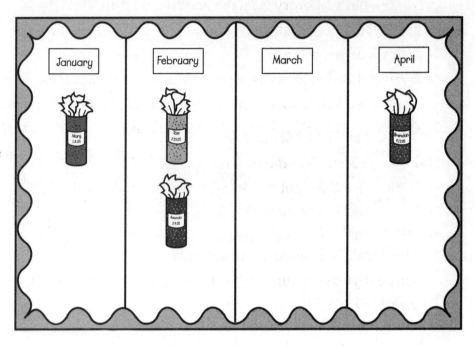

## Directions

***Teacher Preparation:*** Cover the bulletin board with craft paper. Add a border and the caption. Draw lines to divide the board into twelve equal columns. Write the months of the year on the blank word cards. Staple the names of the months at the tops of the columns. Cut index cards into fourths. Cut tissue paper into six-inch squares. Set up a paint station.

1. Invite children to paint a tissue roll with tempera paint to make a candle. Clip a clothespin on one side of the roll for children to hold while they paint.

2. Have them shake glitter on the roll while the paint is wet. Set aside to dry.

3. Have children gently put two or three squares of yellow tissue paper in one end of the roll for the candle flame.

4. Then have them write or dictate their name and their birth date on an index card.

5. Glue or tape the label on the "candle."

6. Staple the birthday candles in the appropriate columns on the bulletin board.

# What Will Happen Next?

***Language Arts Standard:*** *Predicts what will happen next using pictures and content for guides*

- Select a birthday story from the book list on page 45.
- Read aloud the title and tell children the name of the author and the illustrator.
- Read aloud, stopping at a selected part of the story.
- Invite children to look at the pictures and predict what will happen next in the story.

# Presents Galore

***Language Arts Standard:*** *Recognizes and names rhyming words*

- Duplicate and cut out the rhyming picture cards (pages 6–8).
- Enlarge and duplicate twelve gifts (p. 53) on construction paper. Color and cut them out.
- Glue a different rhyming picture from each pair on the back of each gift. Laminate the gifts and the remaining rhyming cards.
- Tape a rhyming picture on the backs on half of the children. Pass out a gift to the remaining half.
- Have children identify the picture on the back of their gifts.
- Then have them find the child whose taped-on picture has a name that rhymes with the name of their picture. The children with the gift should then give it to the partner they have found.
- Encourage partners to name their rhyming words.
- Invite children to switch roles and repeat the activity.

# Looking at Letters and Words

***Language Arts Standard:*** *Begins to identify onsets and rimes*

- Say the following words, separating the onset and rime.

  **c-ake**
  **g-ifts**
  **h-ats**
  **c-andle**
  **g-ames**
  **c-ard**

- Invite children to blend the sounds together and say each word.

Sensational Seasons: Winter, SV 9781419033964

# More or Fewer Candles

**Math Standard:** *Begins to compare groups and recognize more than, less than, and equal to relationships*

- Gather two large number cubes and a dozen birthday candles.
- Cut out a twelve-inch circle from brown felt and another one from pink felt.
- Lay the two circles on the floor and have children sit in a circle around them.
- Explain that the circles are a chocolate and a strawberry birthday cake and that the children are going to help put candles on the cakes.
- Invite a child to sit by each cake and have each child roll one of the number cubes.
- Have each child say aloud the number the cube lands on and put that number of candles on the cake.
- Challenge children to tell which cake has more candles, which has fewer, or if they have the same number.
- Repeat the procedure until all children have had a turn to sit by a cake.

# In Tune with Language

**Language Arts Standard:** *Acts out plays, stories, or songs*

- Have children stand and make a circle around the birthday child.
- Invite children to learn the following song to the tune of "Here We Go 'Round the Mulberry Bush."

   **Here we go 'round the birthday boy,**
   **The birthday boy, the birthday boy.**
   **Here we go 'round the birthday boy.**
   **James is four today.**

- Substitute the appropriate name, gender, and age for each child.
- Have children do the movements for additional verses.

   **Let's clap our hands for the birthday boy...**
   **Let's jump up and down for the birthday boy...**

# Let's Write: Sand Letters

***Language Arts Standard:*** *Writes to produce letters of the alphabet*

- Write the words *Happy Birthday* on a sentence strip and place it on the writing table.

- Provide children with a supply of folded construction paper in several colors, along with stickers, stamps and stamp pads, and markers or crayons.

- Show children a few birthday cards that were purchased at a store.

- Discuss with them how people send birthday cards to help a person celebrate his or her birthday.

- Have children select a favorite storybook character, a pet, a friend, or a family member to make a birthday card for.

- Invite children to write the words *Happy Birthday* on the front of a card and decorate it.

- Have children write the name of the person or pet to whom the card will be given. Have children sign their name on the inside of the card.

# Tiny Birthday Cakes

***Language Arts Standard:*** *Listens with understanding and responds to directions*

- Use a sharp knife to cut small birthday candles in half so that each child has one-half of a candle.

- Provide each child with three plain wafer cookies and a jumbo craft stick on a paper plate. Put a tablespoon of white cake icing and a tablespoon of chocolate cake icing on each child's plate.

- Tell children that they are going to make their own "Tiny Birthday Cake" and that they need to listen so that they will know what to do.

- Invite children to stack their cookies like layers of a cake.

- Have them spread icing between each layer and on the top.

- Have children stick their candle on the top of their "cake."

- Encourage them to sing "Happy Birthday" to themselves.

**Caution: Be aware of children who may have food allergies.**

## Math Center

*Math Standard:*
*Counts objects using one-to-one correspondence*

# How Many Candles on the Cake?

- Duplicate ten cakes (p. 52) on white construction paper. Color and cut them out.

- Write a number from 1 to 10 on each cake. Glue the cakes to poster board squares and laminate them for durability.

- Put about 70 small birthday candles in a container next to the birthday cakes.

- Invite children to count the correct number of candles for each birthday cake.

## Language Center

*Language Arts Standard:*
*Begins to distinguish letters in written text*

# Birthday Words

- Duplicate, color, and cut out the birthday pictures (p. 53).

- Glue each picture in the middle of a colorful, birthday paper plate.

- Put a set of plastic letters or small letter cards in a container next to the plates.

- Invite children to use the letters to spell the names of the birthday pictures. Have children put the letters on the plates with the pictures or on the table next to the plates.

## Art Center

**Language Arts Standard:**
*Uses scribbles, approximations of letters, or known letters to represent written language*

# My Birthday Place Mat

- Provide each child with a large sheet of his or her favorite color of construction paper.
- Invite children to write or dictate the sentence _____'s birthday is _____ at the bottom of the paper.

- Have them cut out a large circle for a face and glue it in the middle of the paper.
- Have them color the face and add features that resemble themselves.
- Then have children draw hair with markers or glue on strips of paper for hair.
- Invite them to decorate the place mat with stickers, glitter, and crayons.
- Laminate the place mats and encourage children to use them at home as a special place setting on their birthday.

## Sensory Center

**Art Standard:**
*Uses responsible procedures in the care and use of materials*

# Make a Cake

- Use your favorite recipe to make white or pink play dough.
- Put a few plastic plates, rolling pins, play dough cutting tools, birthday candles, and plastic candleholders with the play dough.
- Invite children to use a rolling pin to flatten a ball of play dough to make a cake. Have them stack three or four layers on a plate.
- Have them put candles on the cake using the candleholders.
- Have children decorate the cake by slightly pressing colorful pony beads into the dough around the top edge. Larger beads should be used with younger children for safety.
- Encourage children to use the proper procedure for cleanup and have them store the dough in a zippered plastic bag.

Sensational Seasons: Winter, SV 9781419033964

# Birthday Cake Pattern

Use with "How Many Candles on the Cake?" on page 50.

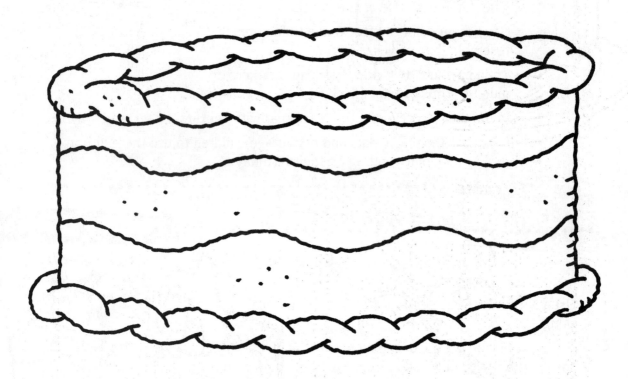

**cake**

# Birthday Patterns

Use with "Presents Galore" on page 47 and "Birthday Words" on page 50.

**cake**

**card**

**hat**

**gift**

**Birthdays: Patterns**
Sensational Seasons: Winter, SV 9781419033964

# Perky Penguins

## Books to Read

*Antarctica* by Helen Cowcher (Farrar, Straus Giroux)

*Cinderella Penguin* by Janet Perlman (Puffin)

*Cuddly Dudley* by Jez Alborough (Candlewick)

*Little Penguin's Tale* by Audrey Wood (Voyager Books)

*Penguin Chick* by Betty Tatham (HarperTrophy)

*Penguin Pete* by Marcus Pfister (North-South)

*Plenty of Penguins* by Sonia Black (Cartwheel)

*Tacky the Penguin* by Helen Lester (Houghton Mifflin/Walter Lorraine Books)

*The Emperor's Egg* by Martin Jenkins (Candlewick)

*The Penguin Family Book* by Lauritz Somme (North-South)

## Penguin Facts

Penguins are one of the few kinds of birds that cannot fly. There are 17 species of penguins. All penguins live in the Southern Hemisphere. The larger species live in the coldest areas. Penguins are excellent swimmers and can stay underwater for several minutes at a time. They are warmblooded animals that are covered with a layer of fat, a layer of down feathers, and a second layer of feathers. Penguins drink salt water from the ocean. They have a special gland in their body that removes the salt from the water and pushes it out of the grooves in their bill. During the mating season, penguins head for a special nesting area on the shore called a rookery. A penguin stays with its mate as long as the pair has a chick. Some male penguins care for their egg while the female leaves in search of food. The male stands with the egg on his feet under a brood pouch for up to nine weeks. He lives off stored fat in his body. The parents recognize their chick by the sound it makes.

Sensational Seasons: Winter, SV 9781419033964

# Playful Penguins

## Materials

- blue and white craft paper
- border
- lunch bags
- newspaper
- black tempera paint
- paintbrushes
- small pieces of white paper
- beak, tummy, and feet patterns (p. 61)
- glue
- pushpins
- markers
- scissors
- stapler

## Directions

***Teacher Preparation:*** Cover the top half of the bulletin board with blue craft paper and the bottom half with white paper. Add the caption and a border. Duplicate the tummy, beak, and feet patterns for each child. Set up a paint center.

1. Have children stuff the lunch bag with strips of newspaper so that the bag is almost full.

2. Have them fold the top of the bag over and tape it down so that it lies flat.

3. Invite children to paint the entire bag black. Set it aside to dry.

4. Have them color the beak and feet orange.

5. Have children cut out the beak, feet, and tummy and glue them on the bag.

6. Encourage them to draw eyes, cut them out, and glue them on the bag.

7. Attach the penguins in a pleasing arrangement using pushpins or staples.

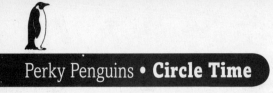
# All About Penguins

***Language Arts Standard:*** *Communicates ideas and thoughts*

- Read aloud an informational book about penguins from the book list on page 54.
- Invite children to tell one thing they learned about penguins from the book. Encourage them to speak in complete sentences.
- Write their sentences on a chart. Point out left to right progression, proper word spacing, capitalization, and punctuation as each sentence is written.
- Use the sentences on the chart with "Penguin Sentences" on page 58.

# Feed the Penguin Chicks

***Language Arts Standard:*** *Matches partner letters*

- Use ten of the completed penguins from "Penguins and Eggs" on page 59 for this activity. Select ten target letters and tape a capital letter on each penguin's tummy.
- Duplicate ten fish (p. 62) on construction paper. Write the partner letters on the back of the fish. Cut out and laminate them.
- Set the penguins on the floor in a line and tell children that these are the penguin chicks.
- Spread the fish, letter side down, on the floor about 10 to 15 feet from the penguins.
- Tell children that penguins often slide on their tummies on the ice into the water to catch food.
- Invite them to help bring the fish to the penguin chicks by matching the partner letters.
- Have children lie on their tummies on a scooter board next to the penguins.
- Have one child at a time roll on the scooter board and catch a fish.
- Then have the child roll back and lay the fish next to the penguin chick that has the partner letter.
- If necessary, spread the fish out again until all children have had a turn.

Sensational Seasons: Winter, SV 9781419033964

# Carry the Egg

**Math Standard:** *Uses positional terms such as in, on, over, or under*

- Discuss with children how the emperor penguins care for their eggs. The mother leaves the egg in search of food and is gone for several weeks. The father keeps the egg warm by holding it on his feet and covering it with a pouch of skin. Whenever he moves, he continues to carry the egg.

- Provide each child with a beanbag.

- Have one child at a time stand and place the beanbag like an egg on his or her feet.

- Tell children to carry their "egg" on their feet and put it in various places around the room such as *on the shelf, under the table, behind the door, in the trash can,* or *between the chairs.*

- Encourage children to say where they put their "egg."

# In Tune with Language

**Language Arts Standard:** *Recognizes and names rhyming words*

- Invite children to learn the following song to the tune of "Itsy Bitsy Spider."

  **The little mother penguin waddled on two legs.**
  **She went to her nest and laid a round egg.**
  **Then she was hungry and wanted to go eat.**
  **So the daddy penguin rolled the egg up on his feet.**

  **He kept the egg warm till the mommy came back.**
  **While he took his turn to eat, the egg began to crack.**
  **Out came a baby chick, fuzzy and gray,**
  **Which made the penguins happy on that special day.**

- Have children identify words that rhyme in the song.

- Write the rhyming words on the board and have children add other words to the list.

# Let's Write: Penguin Sentences

*Language Arts Standard:* *Begins to understand correct punctuation, capitalization, and sentence structure*

• Copy children's sentences from "All About Penguins" on page 56 on strips of paper.

• Have children watch as the words in their sentences are cut apart.

• Invite children to glue the words across the bottom of a sheet of drawing paper. Have them look at the chart for the correct word order and the correct use of capitalization and punctuation.

• Have children draw a picture to illustrate their sentence.

# Cookie Penguins

*Math Standard:* *Names common shapes*

• Twist off one side of a chocolate cookie with white cream filling for each child. Break the plain side into two equal parts.

• Provide children with the cookie half with the cream filling, two broken pieces, and a second whole cookie on a paper plate.

• Invite children to make a penguin on their plate with the whole cookie as the head and the one with the cream filling as the body.

• Have them place the broken cookie halves next to the body for the wings.

• Have children use a small amount of white frosting in a tube to stick on chocolate chips for eyes and an orange jelly bean for the beak.

• Then have them stick two orange jelly beans on for the feet.

• Draw a circle, square, triangle, and rectangle on the board. Have children name the shapes.

• Challenge children to identify any shapes they see on their penguin cookie.

**Caution: Be aware of children who may have food allergies.**

**www.harcourtschoolsupply.com**

**Penguins: Writing Activity and Snack Idea**
Sensational Seasons: Winter, SV 9781419033964

## Math Center

*Math Standard:*
*Uses concepts that include number recognition and counting*

# Walking on Ice

- Cut ten sheets of white construction paper in the shape of ice chunks. Write a number from 1 to 10 on each one. Laminate them and tape them to the floor in a cluster with the numbers in random order.

- Invite children to hold a beanbag between their knees so that they can move like a penguin.

- Have children stand on the number 1.

- Have children hop from chunk to chunk in numerical order.

## Language Center

*Language Arts Standard:*
*Matches partner letters*

# Penguins and Eggs

- Duplicate several penguins and the same number of eggs (p. 62) on construction paper. Color the penguins.

- Write a capital letter on the penguin's tummy and the partner letter on an egg. Cut out and laminate them.

- Invite children to match the partner letters by putting the eggs with the penguins.

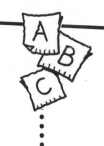

Sensational Seasons: Winter, SV 9781419033964

## Art Center

**Art Standard:**
*Explores a variety
of tools to create
original work*

# Thumbprint Penguins

- Invite children to press their index finger on a black ink pad and print several fingerprint penguin bodies on a half sheet of white paper.

- Have children dip the eraser end of a pencil in white paint and press it in the middle of each fingerprint for the penguin's tummy.

- Have children use a black fine-tip marker to add two black dots on each fingerprint for penguin eyes.

- Then have children dip the end of a toothpick in orange paint and make a tiny dot for the penguin's beak. Have them add two dots for the penguin's feet.

## Science Center

**Science Standard:**
*Uses senses to observe
and explore materials*

# Waxy Feathers

- Discuss with children how penguins have an oil gland from which they extract oil to cover their feathers. Since penguins spend up to 75 percent of their time in the water searching for food, they need this oil to waterproof their bodies.

- Provide each child with one-fourth of a sheet of black construction paper.

- Have children press hard on a white crayon to color half of their black paper.

- Challenge children to fill an eyedropper with water and squeeze drops of water onto each half of the paper.

- Have them compare the water drops on the waxy half with those on the plain areas of paper.

# Beak, Tummy, and Feet Patterns

Use with "Playful Penguins" on page 55.

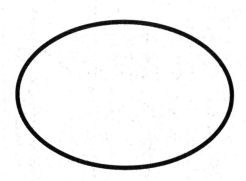

**tummy**

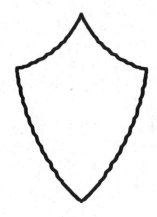

**beak**

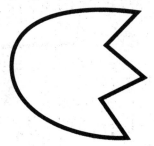 

**feet**

# Penguin, Fish, and Egg Patterns

Use with "Feed the Penguin Chicks" on page 56 and "Penguins and Eggs" on page 59.

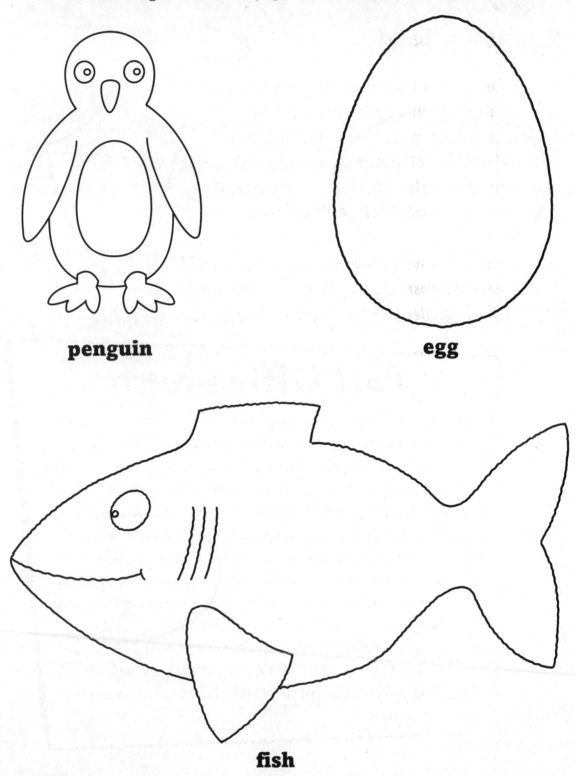

**penguin**

**egg**

**fish**

**Penguins: Patterns**
Sensational Seasons: Winter, SV 9781419033964

## Books to Read

*A Day with a Mail Carrier* by Jan Kottke (Children's Press)

*Dear Annie* by Judith Caseley (HarperTrophy)

*Dear Peter Rabbit* by Alma Flor Ada (Aladdin)

*How It Happens at the Post Office* by Dawn Frederick (Clara House Books)

*The Jolly Postman* by Janet and Allan Ahlberg (Little, Brown Young Readers)

*The Post Office Book: Mail and How It Moves* by Gail Gibbons (HarperTrophy)

*To the Post Office with Mama* by Sue Farrell (Annick Press)

*Will Goes to the Post Office* by Olof Landstrom (R & S Books)

*With Love, Little Red Hen* by Alma Flor Ada (Atheneum)

## Post Office Facts

The U.S. Postal Service processes and delivers mail to individuals and businesses throughout the United States. Post offices are facilities where the public can purchase postage stamps for mailing correspondence or merchandise. A postage stamp is used as evidence of pre-payment for postal services. Usually the postage stamp is a small paper rectangle that is attached to an envelope. Customers can also drop off or pick up packages or other special delivery items. Post offices also rent post-office boxes to people and businesses that prefer not to have mail delivered to their home or office. Mail is processed for delivery in the back rooms of the post offices. There are many separate locations where mail is processed that are not open to the general public. Mail is delivered to individuals and to businesses by mail carriers.

Sensational Seasons: Winter, SV 9781419033964

# Letters for the Mail Carrier

## Materials

- craft paper
- border
- white drawing paper
- crayons or markers
- construction paper
- glue
- stapler

## Directions

***Teacher Preparation:*** Cover the bulletin board with craft paper. Add a border and the caption.

**1.** Read aloud *The Jolly Postman* by Janet and Allan Ahlberg.

**2.** Lead a discussion with children about the storybook characters to which the mail carrier delivers letters.

**3.** Have children write or dictate a brief letter to their favorite storybook character.

**4.** Invite children to draw a picture of their favorite character.

**5.** Have children frame the drawings and the letters by gluing them on construction paper.

**6.** Staple the pictures in a pleasing arrangement on the bulletin board.

# Learning About the Post Office

**Language Arts Standard:** *Relates prior knowledge to new information*

- Make a KWL chart showing three columns. Write the words *KNOW, WANT to know*, and *LEARNED* as headers for each column.
- Have children tell things they know about the post office and mail carriers. Write their responses in the KNOW column.
- Write things children say they want to know about the topics in the WANT column. Guide children to ask questions such as *Who puts letters in the mailbox?*
- Read aloud to children an informational book about the post office from the book list on page 63.
- Invite children to complete the LEARNED column of the chart by telling things that they learned about the post office after you read the book to them. Write their responses in the column.

# Checking Zip Codes

**Math Standard:** *Sorts objects by one or two attributes*

- Collect junk mail, magazines, or catalogs that have been sent to three or four different zip codes.
- Write each zip code on a card and tape it to the end of a box lid or tub.
- Read aloud a book from the list on page 63 that tells about how zip codes are used to help sort the mail.
- Place all of the collected mail in a pile next to the boxes in front of children.
- Invite children to take a piece of mail and find the zip code on it.
- Have children put the mail in the box or tub with the correct zip code.

# Looking at Letters and Words

**Language Arts Standard:** *Demonstrates an understanding of letters and words*

- Make two word cards for each child with the word *stamp* on both of them. Leave about an inch between each letter.
- Give children one of the word cards and have them identify the beginning sound of the word *stamp*.
- Have children count the letters in the word.
- Invite children to cut the letters apart on the second word card and mix them up.
- Encourage children to spell the word *stamp* by looking at the first word card as a model.

# Mail Carrier's Bag

**Language Arts Standard:** *Follows two-step requests that are sequential but not related*

- Make a mailbag from a brown grocery bag. Cut off the top half of the bag on three sides, leaving the back side of the bag for the flap. Use the piece that was removed from the bag to cut straps. Staple a shoulder strap on the sides to complete the mailbag. Write *U.S. MAIL* on the front side of the bag.

- Write two simple directions such as *walk to the door* and *clap your hands two times* on a sheet of paper. Duplicate the sheets to have one for each child. Put each paper inside an envelope. Provide each child with an envelope that has directions in it. Put all of the letters in the mailbag.

- Have children sit in a circle. Choose a volunteer to be the mail carrier and have him or her deliver one letter at a time to children.

- Invite children to open their envelope. Read aloud the "letter" to them.

- Encourage children to follow the directions stated in their "letter."

# In Tune with Language

**Language Arts Standard:** *Begins to distinguish words in sentences*

- Write the following song twice on sentence strips. Put one sentence strip in a pocket chart. Cut the second sentence apart, separating the words. Put each word in a separate envelope. Put all of the envelopes in a basket.

- Invite children to learn the following song to the tune of "A Tisket, a Tasket."

  **A tisket, a tasket,**
  **A pretty little basket.**
  **I wrote a letter to my friend.**
  **And on the way, I dropped it.**

- Have children sit in a circle in front of the pocket chart.

- Pass out a "letter" to each child as the children sing the song.

- Invite them to take turns opening their "letter" and looking at their word.

- Have children put their word card in the pocket chart in front of or below the word that matches it. Some children may need to open two letters, depending on the number of children in the class.

# Let's Write: Picture Postcards

***Language Arts Standard:*** *Uses drawing and writing skills to convey meaning and information*

- Invite children to look at picture postcards that are from interesting places. Show them the picture on one side and the space on the other side for a message.

- Make postcards on large index cards by drawing a line down the middle of one side of the card. Draw a box to indicate where the stamp goes and lines for the address. Leave the message side blank.

- Provide children with blank index postcards, stickers, markers, and old stamps or seals that sometimes come with advertisements.

- Invite children to decorate the blank side of a postcard using the stickers and markers.

- Then have them write or dictate a message and sign their name.

- Have children write or dictate the name of the person in the classroom for whom they are making the card and add a stamp or seal.

- Encourage children to take turns role-playing a mail carrier and deliver the postcards to the class.

# Surprise Package

***Language Arts Standard:*** *Understands that different text forms are used for different purposes*

- Put any kind of snack that does not need to be refrigerated, such as cookies, in a box. Include a short letter to the class that tells them that this is a special snack just for them. To make it more exciting, sign the letter with the name of a friend or family member. It does not really matter who sent the package.

- Wrap the box with brown paper. Tape a canceled stamp on it and address it to you and your class in care of your school.

- Tell children that this package was delivered to them. Invite children to help open it.

- Read the letter, explain who it is from, and pass out the snack.

- Have children help write a thank-you note to the "person" who sent the snack. Have them watch as you address the letter and add a stamp.

- Tell them that you will take it to the post office and mail it for them.

**Caution: Be aware of children who may have food allergies.**

---

**Post Office: Writing Activity and Snack Idea**
Sensational Seasons: Winter, SV 9781419033964

## Math Center

*Math Standard:*
*Recognizes and names numbers*

# Numbers on the Addresses

- Duplicate eight houses and eight letters (p. 70) on construction paper. Color the houses and write a different three-number sequence above the door of each one. Cut them out and laminate them.

- Write the same three-number sequences on the letters and laminate them.

- Discuss with children how every house or building has a number on it to help the mail carriers deliver the mail.

- Invite children to spread out the houses and deliver the correct letter to each house by matching the numbers.

- Encourage children to say aloud the numbers in each sequence.

## Language Center

*Language Arts Standard:*
*Shows awareness that different words begin with the same sound*

# Post-Office Boxes

- Cut the tops off six half-gallon milk cartons and wash the cartons thoroughly. Staple the milk cartons together to make mail slots that have two rows with three cartons in each row. Label the slots with the letters *B, D, M, L, S, T*.

- Duplicate the pictures (p. 71) and cut them out. Glue them on index cards and laminate them for durability.

- Invite children to sort the cards into the correct mail slot by identifying the beginning sound of the name of each picture.

- Encourage children to draw additional pictures on blank cards and deliver them to the correct mail slots.

## Art Center

**Language Arts Standard:**
*Writes to produce letters of the alphabet*

# Mail Truck

- Provide each child with a five-by-six-inch rectangle and a three-by-three-inch square traced on white construction paper.

- Invite children to cut out the shapes and glue them on manila paper to resemble a mail truck.

- Help them trace and cut out 2 three-inch circles from black construction paper and glue them on the truck for wheels.

- Invite children to draw an open door on the truck with a steering wheel and a seat.

- Encourage them to use a red marker to write *U.S. MAIL* on the side of the truck.

- Have children draw a background scene using crayons or markers.

## Science Center

**Math Standard:**
*Uses measuring implements*

# Weighing Packages

- Collect five or six bath soap boxes or empty milk cartons. Put a rock inside each box or carton so that some boxes weigh the same and others are different weights.

- Flatten the ends of the milk cartons and tape them down. Wrap the boxes with brown paper so that they look like packages.

- Tell children that postal workers can tell how much a package costs to mail by weighing it first.

- Provide children with a pan balance and the "packages."

- Invite them to weigh two packages at a time to see which one is heavier or if they weigh the same.

Sensational Seasons: Winter, SV 9781419033964

# House and Letter Patterns

Use with "Numbers on the Addresses" on page 68.

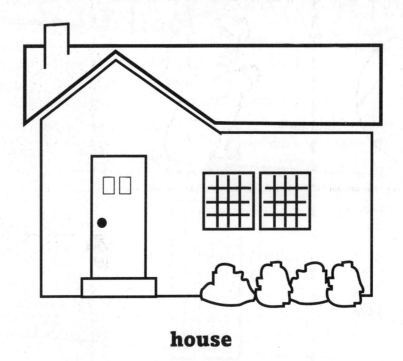

**house**

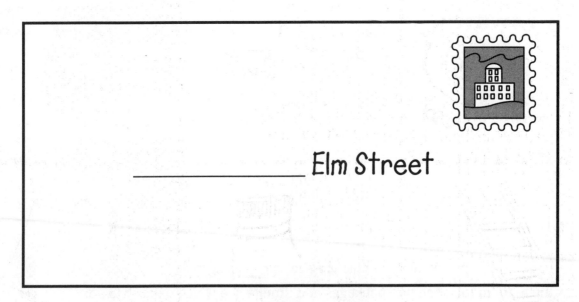

_____ Elm Street

**letter**

# Alphabet Pictures

Use with "Post-Office Boxes" on page 68.

# Valentine's Day

## Books to Read

*A Circle Is Not a Valentine* by H. Werner Zimmerman (Fitzhenry & Whiteside Limited)

*Arthur's Valentine* by Marc Brown (Little, Brown Young Readers)

*Franklin's Valentines* by Paulette Bourgeois (Scholastic Paperbacks)

*Little Mouse's Big Valentine* by Thacher Hurd (HarperTrophy)

*The Day It Rained Hearts* by Felicia Bond (Laura Geringer)

*The Night Before Valentine's Day* by Natasha Wing (Grosset & Dunlap)

*The Story of Valentine's Day* by Nancy Skarmeas (Candy Cane Press)

*The Very Special Valentine* by Maggie Kneen (Chronicle Books)

*What Is Valentine's Day?* by Harriet Ziefert (Sterling)

## Valentine's Day Facts

Valentine's Day is celebrated each year on February 14 and is a day to display affection. It is customary to send cards, called valentines, to friends, family, and loved ones. It is generally believed that Valentine's Day was named for the Roman priest Valentine. An emperor said that no soldier could marry because having a family was a distraction. Valentine defied the ruler and married young soldiers and their sweethearts anyway. Valentine was put to death on February 14 for disobeying the emperor. The early Catholic Church made Valentine a saint. They declared that February 14 would be a day to remember all saints, but today people remember only the story of Valentine.

Sensational Seasons: Winter, SV 9781419033964

# I Love You with All My Heart

## Materials

- blue craft paper
- border
- completed hearts from "Valentine Party Decorations" on page 78
- pink or red construction paper
- glue
- scissors
- stapler
- pencil

## Directions

***Teacher Preparation:*** Cover the bulletin board with craft paper. Add a border and the caption.

**1.** Trace around children's hand with their fingers separated.

**2.** Have children cut out their handprint.

**3.** Invite children to fold down and glue the middle and ring finger on the paper handprint to resemble the hand sign for "I love you."

**4.** Have children glue the handprint in the middle of the finger-painted heart.

**5.** Have them glue the heart on red or pink construction paper.

**6.** Help children cut around the heart shape through both thicknesses so that the construction paper frames the heart.

**7.** Arrange the hearts in a pleasing arrangement on the bulletin board.

Sensational Seasons: Winter, SV 9781419033964

# Valentine Letter Hunt

**Language Arts Standard:** *Begins to distinguish letters in written text*

• Write the words *HAPPY VALENTINE'S DAY* on the board in large uppercase letters.

• Duplicate eighteen hearts (p. 79) on red construction paper. Write a letter from the words *HAPPY VALENTINE'S DAY* on each heart. Cut out the hearts and laminate them for durability.

• Hide the hearts, letter side down, around the room so that children can easily find them.

• Invite children to find a heart and sit in front of the board.

• Read the words to children. Then point to one letter at a time following left to right sequence.

• Have the child who has the same letter that you are pointing to use double-sided tape to stick it directly below that letter on the board. If two children have the same letter, help them find where they both should be placed.

• Challenge children to read aloud the words when all of the letters have been placed on the board.

• You may wish to include other valentine words such as *BE MINE* if there are more than eighteen children in the group.

# Whose Valentine Is This?

**Language Arts Standard:** *Identifies letters in own name*

• Purchase an inexpensive box of valentine cards and envelopes so that there is one card and one envelope for each child.

• Write each child's name on an envelope.

• Write a target letter on the backs of half of the cards.

• Then write the partner letters on the backs of the remaining cards.

• Put each valentine card in an envelope.

• Have children identify their name as the envelopes are held up one at a time. Pass out the envelopes as children identify their name.

• Invite children to open their envelope and look at the letter on the back of the card.

• Have them find and sit with the child who has the card with their partner letter.

• Encourage partners to say their letter aloud.

# Counting Hearts

**Math Standard:** *Explores quantity and number*

- Put 10 to 20 heart-shaped erasers in a small, clear jar. If children have had previous experience with estimation, the number of erasers can be greater.
- Cut out a four-inch pink heart from construction paper for each child.
- Invite children to guess or estimate how many hearts are in the jar.
- Write children's names and their guesses on the paper hearts.
- Tape all of the hearts on the board or on a wall where children can see them.
- Have children help count the hearts in the jar.
- Challenge children to look at a number line to determine whose guess was the closest to the correct amount.
- Have the child who had the best guess pass out a heart eraser to each child.

# In Tune with Language

**Language Arts Standard:** *Recognizes and names rhyming words*

- Invite children to learn the following poem.

**Five little valentines were having a race.**
**The first little valentine was frilly with lace.**
**The second little valentine had a funny face.**
**The third little valentine said, "I love you!"**
**The fourth little valentine said, "I do, too."**
**The fifth little valentine was sly as a fox.**
**He ran the fastest to the valentine box.**

- Challenge children to name words in the poem that rhyme.

# Let's Write: Heart-Shaped Candy Box

**Language Arts Standard:** *Writes to produce letters of the alphabet*

- Glue the paper candy wrappers from an empty heart-shaped box of candy inside the box. Stick a white sticker dot to the center of each candy wrapper. Write a target letter on each sticker. Sight words may be written instead of letters.

- Use clay to make balls of "candy" that fit inside each candy wrapper to cover the letters or sight words. Discuss with children that this is clay and not real candy.

- Duplicate the candy box activity master (p. 80) for each child.

- Invite children to remove a piece of "candy" from the box and set it aside.

- Then have them write on their paper the letter that is revealed.

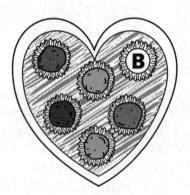

- Encourage children to continue removing candy pieces and writing letters until their candy box activity master is full.

- Have them replace the "candy" in the box so that it can be used again.

# Valentine Bagels

**Math Standard:** *Counts objects using one-to-one correspondence*

- Provide children with a tablespoon of softened cream cheese in a paper cup and a jumbo craft stick. Squeeze a few drops of red food coloring into the cup.

- Invite children to mix the food coloring with the cream cheese until it is pink.

- Have them spread the cream cheese on a bagel that has been cut in half.

- Then have children decorate the bagel with red candies.

- Challenge them to count how many red candies they put on their bagel.

**Caution: Be aware of children who may have food allergies.**

Sensational Seasons: Winter, SV 9781419033964

## Math Center

**Math Standard:**
*Begins to order objects in some attribute*

# Hoppin' Hearts

- Cut out and laminate six hearts of different sizes from red construction paper.

- Tape the hearts on the floor so that they are close enough so that children can safely jump to each one no matter on which heart they stand.

- Invite children to take turns hopping to the hearts in order from the smallest to the largest or from the largest to the smallest.

## Language Center

**Language Arts Standard:**
*Matches partner letters*

# Broken Hearts

- Duplicate the heart (p. 79) for use as a template. Trace and cut out eight hearts on red or pink poster board. Cut each heart in half using a different puzzle cut.

- Write eight target letters on the hearts with the capital letters on one half and the partner letters on the matching half.

- Invite children to piece the heart puzzles together by matching the partner letters.

## Art Center

*Art Standard:*
*Explores a variety of techniques to create original work*

# Valentine Party Decorations

- Discuss with children how two colors can be mixed together to make a third color.
- Invite them to mix together red and white finger paint on white paper. Encourage them to cover the entire paper with paint.
- Have them find the pink areas that they made.
- When the paint is dry, use a black marker to draw a large heart shape on their painting.
- Have children cut out the heart shape and use it as a room decoration.
- Then have them glue the remaining part of the painting with the missing heart cutout to a piece of red construction paper. Laminate it and use it as a place mat.

## Sensory Center

*Math Standard:*
*Describes and extends simple patterns*

# Sandy Heart Patterns

- Use a spray bottle of water to dampen the sand in the sand table.
- Provide children with a variety of sizes of heart cookie cutters.
- Invite partners to take turns making patterns in the sand using the cookie cutters.
- Have one child make a pattern by pressing the cutters into the sand while the partner faces away.
- Then have the partner look at the pattern, describe it aloud, and reproduce it.

Sensational Seasons: Winter, SV 9781419033964

# Heart Pattern
Use with "Valentine Letter Hunt" on page 74 and "Broken Hearts" on page 77.

**heart**

**Valentines: Pattern**
Sensational Seasons: Winter, SV 9781419033964

**Name**

# Candy Box

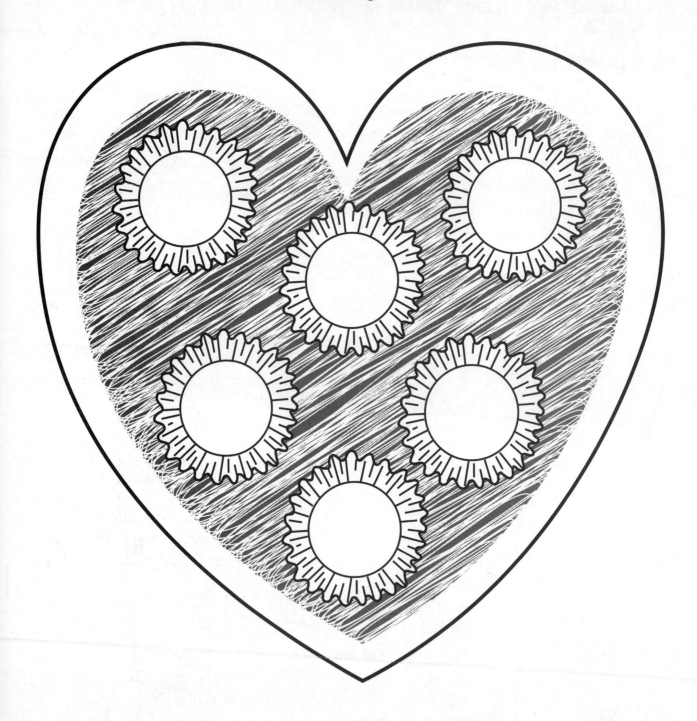

***Directions:*** Use with "Heart-Shaped Candy Box" on page 76. Invite children to write a letter in each section of the candy box.

Sensational Seasons: Winter, SV 9781419033964

# Brush Up on Dental Health

## Books to Read

*Arthur's Tooth* by Marc Brown (Little, Brown Young Readers)

*Brush Well: A Look at Dental Care* by Katie Bagley (Capstone Press)

*Brush Your Teeth Please* by Leslie McGuire (Reader's Digest)

*Going to the Dentist* by Anne Civardi (Usborne Books)

*How Many Teeth?* by Paul Showers (HarperCollins)

*Nice Try, Tooth Fairy* by Mary W. Olson (Aladdin Books)

*Rotten Teeth* by Laura Simms (Houghton Mifflin)

*Tooth Fairy* by Audrey Wood (Child's Play International Limited)

*What Do Fairies Do with All Those Teeth?* By Michel Luppens (Scholastic)

## Teeth Facts

Teeth are used to bite and chew food. Different teeth have different jobs. Incisor teeth, in the front of the mouth, are used for grasping. Canine teeth are sharp and are used for tearing foods such as meat. Molars are big and flat teeth that are good for mashing and grinding food. People have two sets of teeth throughout their lives. Children have 20 primary teeth that are replaced with permanent teeth by about age 13. Adults have 32 teeth. Proper brushing, flossing, and regular dental care are needed to prevent plaque, which is a transparent layer of bacteria that coats the teeth. If plaque is not removed from the teeth, then cavities, or holes, can form in the enamel of teeth.

Sensational Seasons: Winter, SV 9781419033964

# Healthy Teeth, Happy Mouth

## Materials

- any color craft paper
- border
- tooth puppet patterns (p. 88)
- paper plates
- red tempera paint
- paintbrushes
- white, blue, and pink construction paper
- mini-marshmallows
- paint containers
- markers
- glue
- scissors
- stapler

## Directions

***Teacher Preparation:*** Cover the bulletin board with craft paper. Add a border and the caption. Duplicate the patterns on construction paper for each child: two white eyes, one blue nose, and one pink tongue.

**1.** Have children fold a plate in half and paint the inside of the plate red.

**2.** Invite children to glue the eyes and nose on one side of the folded plate. Have them use a marker to draw pupils in the eyes.

**3.** Have children glue the tongue on the inside of the plate.

**4.** Tell children to glue the marshmallows along the inside top and bottom rims of the plate for teeth.

**5.** Have children set their puppet aside to dry.

**6.** Staple the tooth puppets in a pleasing arrangement on the bulletin board.

# The Dentist Office

***Language Arts Standard:*** *Retells information from a story*

• Select a book about visiting the dentist from the book list on page 81.

• Read aloud the title and tell children the name of the author and the illustrator.

• Point out where the story starts and then read the book aloud.

• Invite children to retell information from the book about visiting a dentist's office.

# Pass the Toothpaste

***Language Arts Standard:*** *Identifies some beginning sounds*

• Duplicate a tooth (p. 89) on white construction paper for each child. Cut out the teeth.

• Select three or four letter sounds to target such as /t/ for tooth. Cut out pictures of objects whose names begin with those sounds and glue one picture on each tooth. Laminate the teeth.

• Invite children to sit in a circle. Place a tooth facedown in front of each child. Tell children that they are the mouth that holds all of the teeth.

• Play music and have children pass a tube of toothpaste around the circle until the music stops.

• Have the children left holding the toothpaste look at the picture on the back of their tooth and identify the beginning sound in its name. Have them put the tooth behind them after their turn because the tooth has "fallen out."

• Repeat the process until all children have had a turn to be left holding the toothpaste. The length of time the music plays before stopping will be determined by which children still need a turn.

# Looking at Letters and Words

***Language Arts Standard:*** *Demonstrates some ability to hear separate syllables in words*

• Write the word *toothpaste* on the board. Have children tell what words they hear in the word *toothpaste* (*tooth* and *paste*).

• Invite children to say the word slowly and segment the syllables (*tooth-paste*).

• Have children clap the syllables as they say them aloud and then blend the word *toothpaste* back together.

• Encourage children to clap and count the syllables for other words such as *teeth, mouth, cavity, molars, incisors,* and *dentist*.

# How Many Teeth?

**Math Standard:** *Solves simple mathematical problems*

- Duplicate a counting board (p. 90) for each child. Color the lips, gums, and tongue. Cut out and laminate them so they can be reused at other times.

- Provide children with a counting board and a small cup of large white lima beans.

- Invite children to count the correct number of bean "teeth" on their counting board to solve the following word problems.

  **You have 4 teeth in your mouth. Then you lose 2 teeth. How many teeth do you have left?**

  **You have 3 teeth on the top and 3 teeth on the bottom. How many teeth do you have altogether?**

  **You have 5 teeth in your mouth. One more tooth is growing in. How many teeth will you have?**

- Continue with other word problems as long as there is interest.

# In Tune with Language

**Language Arts Standard:** *Understands that reading progresses from left to right*

- Write the words to the song below on a chart.

  **I brush my teeth each day.**
  **I brush my teeth each day.**
  **I brush my teeth each day.**
  **To keep away decay.**
  **To keep away decay.**
  **To keep away decay.**
  **I brush my teeth each day.**
  **To keep away decay.**

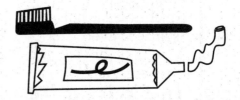

- Invite children to learn the song to the tune of "The Bear Went over the Mountain."

- Use a pointer to point to each word as it is sung, emphasizing left to right progression.

# Let's Write: Dear Tooth Fairy

**Language Arts Standard:** *Understands that different text forms are used for different purposes*

- Read aloud the book *Tooth Fairy* by Audrey Wood.

- Lead a discussion with children about why they put their teeth under their pillow for the tooth fairy.

- Invite children to write or dictate a letter to the tooth fairy.

- Have them draw a picture of the tooth fairy with their letter.

- Encourage them to put the letter under their pillow next time they lose a tooth.

> Dear Tooth Fairy,
> Here is my tooth.
> Thank you for the money.
>
> Love,
> Hope

# Healthy Teeth Kabobs

**Math Standard:** *Describes and extends simple patterns*

- Provide a bowl of seedless grapes that have been washed, a bowl of banana slices, a bowl of pineapple chunks, and a bowl of cheese cubes.

- Lead a discussion with children about foods that are healthy for their teeth.

- Invite children to place the foods on a kabob stick in a pattern such as cheese, grape, banana, pineapple, cheese, grape, banana, pineapple.

- Have children describe their pattern to a classmate.

- Have children carefully pull off one piece at a time from the kabob stick. Encourage them to notice how they use their molars for chewing as they eat each piece.

**Caution: Be aware of children who may have food allergies.**

Sensational Seasons: Winter, SV 9781419033964

## Math Center

*Math Standard:*
*Counts objects using one-to-one correspondence*

# Counting Teeth

- Duplicate ten counting boards (p. 90) on construction paper. Color and cut them out.

- Write a number from 1 to 10 in the corner of each counting board. Laminate the boards.

- Purchase about 60 one-inch white ceramic tiles from a hardware or home decorating store to use as teeth. Often stores will give odd tiles for free. If tiles are not available, cut white poster board into one-inch squares. Put the tiles or squares in a small container.

- Invite children to count the correct number of "teeth" tiles on each board.

# Toothy Words

## Language Center

*Language Arts Standard:*
*Begins to recognize high-frequency words*

- Duplicate several teeth (p. 89) on white construction paper. Cut them out.

- Write a familiar high-frequency word on each tooth and laminate them. Stick a small piece of magnetic tape on the back of each tooth.

- Provide children with the paper teeth with words, a metal cookie sheet, and a set of magnetic letters.

- Invite them to stick one tooth on the cookie sheet.

- Have them spell the word using the magnetic letters.

- For younger children, write letters of the alphabet on the teeth and have them find the magnetic letters that match.

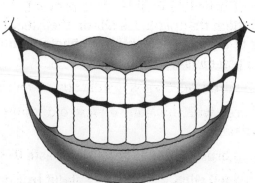

## Art Center

**Art Standard:**
*Explores a variety of techniques to create original work*

# Dental Floss Painting

- Use a tooth (p. 89) as a guide for drawing a large tooth on white construction paper for each child.
- Have children cut out the tooth.
- Invite them to dip a twelve-inch piece of dental floss in tempera paint.
- Help children lay the painted string on the paper tooth, making sure to leave the end hanging free.
- Have them repeat the procedure with one or two other pieces of dental floss that are dipped in other colors of paint.
- Have children cover the tooth and the strings with another sheet of paper.
- Hold the top paper in place while children pull the strings out one at a time.
- Remove the top piece of paper to reveal the string painting.

## Science Center

**Language Arts Standard:**
*Communicates information with others*

# "Egg-stra" Good Brushing

- Lead a discussion with children about the importance of brushing their teeth to prevent plaque. Tell them that plaque is left on their teeth after eating or drinking. It mixes with bacteria (germs) and can cause cavities.
- Soak several hard-boiled eggs in cola soda overnight.
- Provide children with the stained eggs, old toothbrushes, and a small tube of toothpaste.
- Invite them to brush the eggs with toothpaste to clean them.
- Have children tell what they learned about brushing their teeth.

# Tooth Puppet Patterns

Use with "Healthy Teeth, Happy Mouth" on page 82.

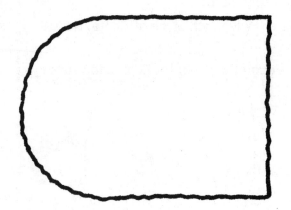

**tongue**

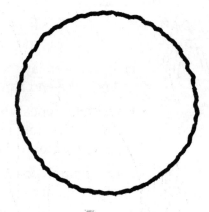

**eye**

**nose**

 Sensational Seasons: Winter, SV 9781419033964

# Teeth Patterns

Use with "Pass the Toothpaste" on page 83, "Toothy Words" on page 86, and "Dental Floss Painting" on page 87.

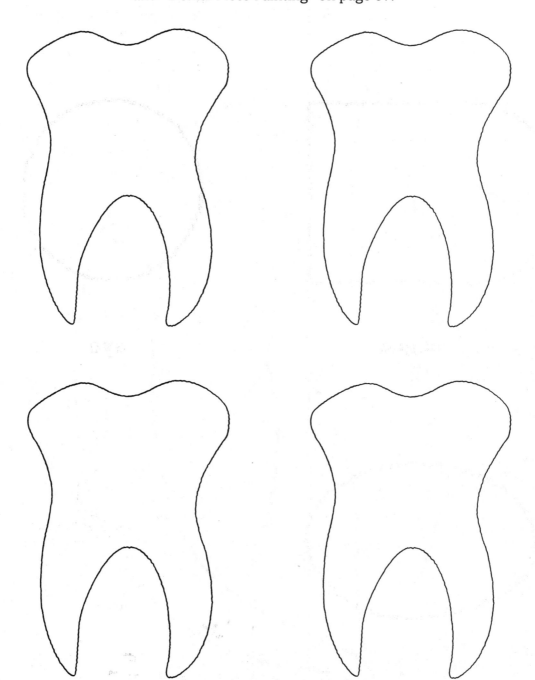

**teeth**

# Mouth Counting Board

Use with "How Many Teeth?" on page 84 and "Counting Teeth" on page 86.

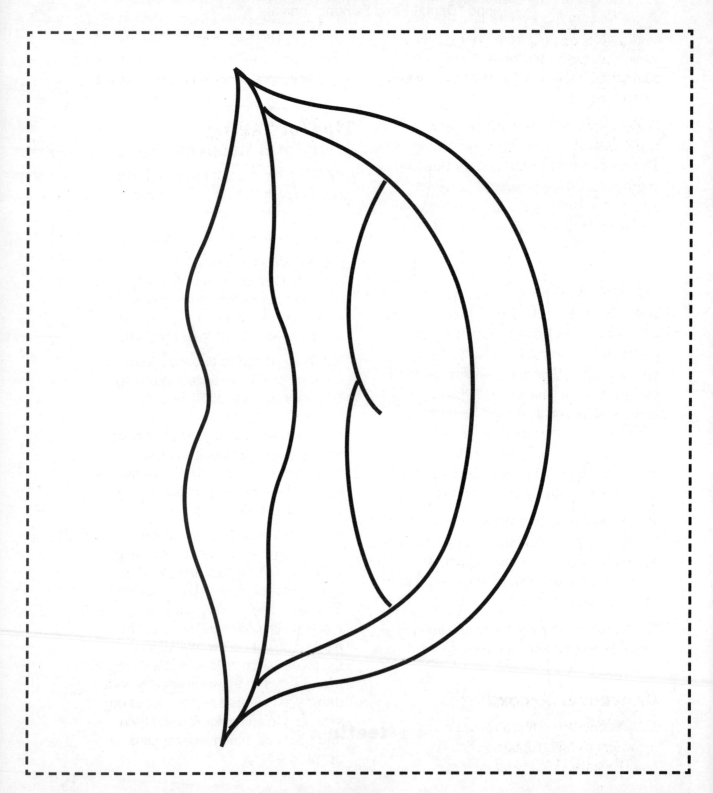

# Assessment

We observe children every day in our classrooms. Most of the time, these observations are done on an informal basis. We may not even realize the valuable information we gain from them. Often we recognize how much we really do know about the children in our classroom when we formally assess them.

Our observations are only the very beginning of assessment in our classrooms. The terms **assessment** and **evaluation** are often used interchangeably, yet assessment must occur before evaluation can take place. To assess means to collect data. To evaluate means to analyze that data.

During our daily observations, we collect data on each of the children in our classrooms. However, to make that assessment worthwhile, it is important to go one step further and evaluate the data that we collect. The key to assessment in our classrooms is the evaluations we make and how we use those evaluations to inform instruction. We cannot just assess children. Without evaluation, the assessment is hardly worth noting.

Just as we create lesson plans for each day, so must we plan assessment opportunities. Assessment does not just happen. In addition, we must plan time for evaluation of the data we collect.

On the following pages, you will find some valuable assessments for your preschoolers.

## Anecdotal Records

An anecdotal record is a record of the behaviors a child exhibits during the day. It tells a story about what the child can do. Over time, anecdotal records create snapshots of the children in your class. Anecdotal records are probably one of the easiest assessment tools to use in your classroom. This tool is an appropriate one to use on a daily basis, and the time devoted to taking anecdotal records is very minimal.

## Tips for Taking Anecdotal Records

- Keep your anecdotal record system close at hand. This will allow you to note behaviors quickly.

- Be sure to date your records.

- Set goals for the number of anecdotal records you will make each day. For instance, every day of the week you may want to make notes on one-fifth of your children.

- It may be helpful to choose a focus for your anecdotal records each day. This may be particularly helpful if you are just beginning to use anecdotal records in your classroom. For example, one week you may want to note what kinds of writing each child is engaged in during writing activities.

- Attempt to keep your anecdotal records positive. Rather than noting what a child ***can't*** do, note what he or she ***can*** do instead. For example, *Today Mary was able to navigate a return sweep while reading her guided reading book.* Don't worry about the fact that the child wasn't able to match the written words entirely with the spoken words. Keep the focus on what children can do. You will then find your instruction also remains positive.

**Assessment**
Sensational Seasons: Winter, SV 9781419033964

- Set aside time at least once a month to review and evaluate your anecdotal records. Note any patterns you find within a group of students or a pattern you see emerging with one particular child.

- Use your anecdotal records to inform your instruction. For instance, if you find a group of children who are continually attempting to write poetry during writing time, you may want to pull them together to talk about various types of poetry writing. If you note a group of children who are having difficulty retelling stories they have read, pull them together in a group to work on retelling simple stories. These examples illustrate the use of anecdotal records to inform your instruction.

## Organizing Anecdotal Records

The following is just one organizational system that can help to make your use of anecdotal records efficient. Write each child's name at the bottom of a 4″ x 6″ ruled index card. Then lay the index cards on a clipboard in a layered effect. Attach the cards with tape.

As you plan your assessment opportunities, keep the clipboard and a pen—which can be attached to the clipboard with a string—with you. Note behaviors you observe on a child's index card. Be sure to date your observations. Plan to note behaviors for at least one-fifth of the children in your class each day. That will allow you to have at least one anecdotal record for each child each week.

As you fill index cards, replace them. File the completed cards in your children's portfolios.

Anecdotal records can be taken for any subject. Be sure not only to date your anecdotal records, but to record the subject matter so you can quickly look through the records and find patterns in a particular subject. Once a month, spend five to ten minutes rereading the anecdotal records on one child. Look for patterns to address in your instruction.

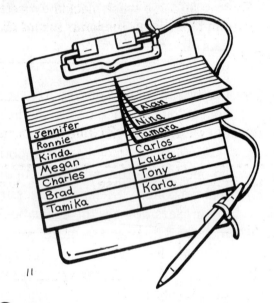

**Assessment**
Sensational Seasons: Winter, SV 9781419033964

# ABC/Phonemic Awareness Assessment

To assess children's alphabet knowledge, copy the ABC assessment card on page 94. Laminate it for durability. Also make copies of the ABC assessment recording sheet on this page. Plan to assess children on their alphabet knowledge a minimum of twice a year, once at the beginning and once at the end.

• • • • • • • • • • • • • • • • • • • • • • • • • • • • • • • • • • • • • • • • •

## Teacher Directions:

- As you call a child over to work with you, show him or her the ABC assessment card. Say to the child: **What are these?** Do not use the word "letters," as you will want to note what the child calls these symbols.

- Show only one row of letters at a time. This will allow children to focus better.

- Point to each letter and say: **Tell me what this is.** The child should tell you the name of the letter. Record the child's response.

- You can also use these blackline masters to assess phonemic awareness. Simply point to each letter and say: **Tell me what sound this letter makes.**

Child's Name: _____ Date: _____

Child's Approximate Age: _____ Child's Score: _____ /54

Ask: **What are these?** Child's response: _____

• • • • • • • • • • • • • • • • • • • • • • • • • • • • • • • • • • • • • • • • •

✔ = **correct response**          x = **incorrect response**          ○ = **no response**

| a ___ | e ___ | i ___ | m ___ | q ___ | u ___ | y ___ |
| b ___ | f ___ | j ___ | n ___ | r ___ | v ___ | z ___ |
| c ___ | g ___ | k ___ | o ___ | s ___ | w ___ | a ___ |
| d ___ | h ___ | l ___ | p ___ | t ___ | x ___ | g ___ |
| A ___ | E ___ | I ___ | M ___ | Q ___ | U ___ | Y ___ |
| B ___ | F ___ | J ___ | N ___ | R ___ | V ___ | Z ___ |
| C ___ | G ___ | K ___ | O ___ | S ___ | W ___ | |
| D ___ | H ___ | L ___ | P ___ | T ___ | X ___ | |

# ABC Assessment Card

a e i m q u y

b f j n r v z

c g k o s w a

d h l p t x g

........................................................................................

A E I M Q U Y

B F J N R V Z

C G K O S W

D H L P T X

**Assessment**
Sensational Seasons: Winter, SV 9781419033964

# Emergent Reading Checklist

## Teacher Directions:

During whole-group, small-group, or independent reading time, observe children as they are engaged in the reading process. Be sure to note a child's reading behavior at least once each quarter during the year. This checklist can also be useful at report card time.

Name: _____ Grade: _____

| | Date of Entries | | | ✔ |
|---|---|---|---|---|
| Enjoys listening to books | | | | |
| Confidently participates in shared reading | | | | |
| Makes meaningful predictions using the story and pictures as clues | | | | |
| Retells stories and rhymes | | | | |
| Approximates book language | | | | |
| Uses pictures to comprehend text | | | | |
| Realizes that print carries a message | | | | |
| Demonstrates book handling skills | | | | |
| Locates the name of the author and illustrator | | | | |
| Recognizes parts of a book (cover, title, title page) | | | | |
| Demonstrates directionality: left to right | | | | |
| Demonstrates directionality: top to bottom | | | | |
| Identifies uppercase and lowercase letters | | | | |
| Demonstrates an understanding of letters and words | | | | |
| Identifies some sounds | | | | |
| Matches spoken words to print | | | | |
| Recognizes own name and common environmental print | | | | |
| Reads some one-syllable and high-frequency words | | | | |
| Chooses to look at/read books from a variety of sources | | | | |
| Can sit still for short periods of time to read a book | | | | |

**Checklist**
Sensational Seasons: Winter, SV 9781419033964

# Emergent Writing Checklist

## Teacher Directions:

Observe children during whole-group writing experiences and independent writing experiences. Be sure to note student writing behavior at least once each quarter during the year. This checklist can also be useful at report card time.

Name: _____ Grade: _____

| | Date of Entries | | | ✔ |
|---|---|---|---|---|
| Makes pre-letter writing marks on paper | | | | |
| Writes letters, symbols, or numerals randomly | | | | |
| Writes some uppercase and lowercase letters of the alphabet | | | | |
| Demonstrates directionality of letters | | | | |
| Writes initial consonants | | | | |
| Writes partially phonetically spelled words | | | | |
| Writes some completely phonetically spelled words | | | | |
| Writes high-frequency words randomly | | | | |
| Writes a few known words correctly | | | | |
| Uses random finger pointing when reading his or her writing | | | | |

**Checklist**
Sensational Seasons: Winter, SV 9781419033964